WITH THE HUCKLEBERRY CHRIST

A Spiritual Journey

Kristen Johnson Ingram

1817

Harper & Row, Publishers, San Francisco

Cambridge, Hagerstown, New York, Philadelphia, Washington
London, Mexico City, São Paulo, Singapore, Sydney

Cover design: Terry Dugan

Scripture texts not otherwise designated are taken from the *Revised Standard Version Common Bible* (here, RSV), copyright © 1973 by the Division of Christian Education of the National Council of the Churches of Christ in the U.S.A. Used by permission. Texts designated NEB are taken from the *New English Bible*, copyright © 1961 and 1970 by Oxford University Press. Used by permission.

Chapter 3, "Huckleberry Christ," was printed in the *Desert Call*, Winter 1979. Reprinted by permission.

In Chapter 6, the line "All I need is the air that I breathe, yes, to love you" is taken from "The Air That I Breathe," by Albert Hammond and Mike Hazlewood, © 1972, 1973, April Music, Inc. International copyright secured. All rights reserved. Used by permission.

Copyright © 1985 by Kristen Johnson Ingram.
All rights reserved. No part of this book may be reproduced in any form without written permission from Winston Press, Inc.

Library of Congress Catalog Card Number: 85-50246

ISBN: 0-86683-798-1

Printed in the United States of America

5 4 3 2

For the word of God is alive and active. It cuts more keenly than any two-edged sword, piercing as far as the place where life and spirit, joints and marrow, divide. It sifts the purposes and thoughts of the heart. There is nothing in creation that can hide from him; everything lies naked and exposed to the eyes of the One with whom we have to reckon. (Hebrews 4:12-13, NEB)

For Susan and Carol and Frank and George and Matthew and Kimberley and Andrew and Adam and Victor and my mother and Nels; and for my friend, Father William McNamara, O.C.D.

CONTENTS

I
THE LORD OF THE DANCE

> You have come to Mount Zion and the city of the living God, the heavenly Jerusalem, and to innumerable angels in festal gathering. (Hebrews 12:22)

When I was a young girl, I planned to grow up and be an archaeologist and an inventor and a great writer and a portrait painter and a harpsichordist and a beauty queen and the mother of at least six superb children. What happened was that I grew old early and grew up late, and I am now middle-aged; and the Mary and Martha in me vie constantly for supremacy.

For instance, this morning I thought, I'll write all morning; and then, No, I'll clean the closets. I fell back to sleep and so did neither, until my daughter called and said she was sick. Andrew, my two-year-old grandson, came to visit, which decided a lot about my day.

But even as Andrew played and scampered and wrought havoc and smeared and charmed me, I was suddenly confronted by Christ.

I was attempting to throw the woven bedspread over last night's sleep, with Andrew's tugging assistance, when Christ was suddenly there, like a moving sunbeam on the walls of my spirit. His eyes shine like Andrew's in their awful clarity; and their innocent vitality jars me for a moment as I realize that his father, our Father, sees us not only with a father's knowing eyes or a father's hope and dream, but also with that careening joy that grandparents pour onto their grandchildren.

As Andrew disrupts my Mary meditation and smears my Martha blue jeans with applesauce, I hold him at arms' length and threaten to do violence to his person if he doesn't stay out of the dog's water; and in the middle of this chastening, I hug him in the throes of overwhelming love.

"God is a grandmother," I say into Andrew's warm, powdered neck, and he holds on for all he is worth, which is considerable.

God is a grandmother, because he has that ridiculously unconditional Love for us. Even as he hastens and chastens his will to make own, he holds my wriggling and sinful soul away from him, and his love comes pouring down from the throne.

"Like treacle?" asks the Dormouse, who lives on the tittering right side of my brain. No, sleepy mouse, more than treacle, more than oil, more than milk and honey. More like the whole sky sieved down into my heart.

I always intend to greet Christ formally when he confronts me as he did this morning; I plan, like Thomas, to bend my knee and gasp, "My Lord and my God!" But instead, I discover myself stockstill before leaping—as stockstill as Andrew is when he looks out the window and sees me assaulting the steep, fir-covered lot in front of their house. He always freezes for a moment, transfixed, at the sight of Grandmother climbing the nineteen steps, with her green Greek bag and perhaps something he has left behind—a ball, a pair of socks—and I can tell that his glassy blue gaze is a part of wondering if I am real at all; and then he just as suddenly focuses and begins to pound the windowsill and shout, "Grannuther!"

Sometimes he throws one arm around El Barko, the long-eared black hound that likes to put her paws on the sill and watch too. They both always beat me to the front door and come tumbling and licking and panting and hugging, just the way I came tumbling to Christ while making the bed.

It's only after my fall from Thomas to Tumbler that I usually get serious again and remember who it is I'm addressing. I start to think of the Tabernacle and the angels crying, "Holy! Holy! Holy! Holy is the Lord!" in constant, overlapping succession: and I remember that he is not just today's gentle friend but the beardless glory that brought me to awe in the Sistine Chapel, his arm upraised in judgment.

Andrew pulled the bedspread back off the bed as I talked long-distance to a friend who may come to visit this summer. I always worry when friends visit from other states: the lush summer green of Oregon, the deep forests, the blue ceonothus overhanging roadside ledges of healing salal, the hot purple vetch, the lakes, and trout leaping for the love of God in their streams— all this sometimes drives people to buy property here.

"It rains and rains here," I tell them, Cassandra in the fir grove. "It rains and rains and rains."

Actually, this city usually gets about forty inches a year, near the same amount as some cities in, say, Kansas; but Kansas gets it all on about six dark, drowning, thunderous days when sheets and sheets of water sometimes make drivers stop their cars at the sides of the road, and sirens whistle the danger of tornadoes that lurk just in front of the pressure ridge.

In Oregon it just rains quietly and gently and relentlessly for nine or ten months, all fall and winter and spring.

Are all prophets? Apostles? Rainmakers? God's message for Oregon is different from the one he has for Kansas or Virginia or Utah. The variety of his messages is endlessly beneficent; but you do need a certain kind of faith to live in the constant, drizzling rain.

When I was a child growing up in Arizona, with sandstone Pickett Post outlining my western horizon, and the dizzying pink pinnacles of Apache Leap on the east, O, when I was a little girl prospecting for copper along the railroad tracks and naming lizards that lay on the smooth green skin of the Palo Verde trees, when I was a child gulping sulfur smoke every day at the four o'clock copper smelting, then the message of God was hotter; harsher, maybe, more easily defined, like the saguaro cactus silhouetted at dawn on the ridge above my bedroom window. The skies and ground are clear in their intent, and the sun warms the soil like sweet breath; but there are scorpions in the cornerstones, and almost every kind of plant has thorns that leap into soft skin.

I dreamed a crucifixion once, but when I looked closer it was not Christ on the cross: it was a scorpion, with his smiting tail pinned down and his lobsterlike pincers armed out, fixed to the crossbars. Although I slept, I cowered at my own imagination, and cried, "Blasphemy!" to my Dreamer. But then I looked some more, and saw it for what it was.

"What was it, then?" asks the Raggedy Ann doll that perches just inside my left ear and whispers childlike questions.

It was Death, Raggedy. It was the devil's own offering, there on the wooden cross outside Jerusalem; it was his ability to kill us; it was the Curse; it was the poisonous tradition that, since Adam and until the cross, said that all must die.

A scorpion on the cross makes for an empty tomb. When Jesus died, death died; when Christ rose, I was somehow, through an act of atonement I cannot put words to, made alive.

And it was sin, Raggedy Ann. Death died and sin died, so the things that funeral directors are busy with are only reminders of our own deliverance.

Raggedy smiles. Her red cotton mouth is spread wide as she says, "Can you not sin, then?"

Oh, can I! I can still sin. But I can't Sin. I know that Sin can kill me forever; but sin can be forgiven.

I will sin a little (if indeed there are degrees of sin) if my Northeastern friend comes to visit, because I somehow won't be able to tell her about the Christ I know. I'll tell her, yes; but somehow in the face of our friendship and her assumed notions, I'll grow inarticulate and sullen about it. She thinks I am trapped by doctrine, and what I cannot seem to say to her is that I am indeed caught—like a fish in a net—by a Person.

And the subject will inevitably get to belief, since she wonders why I persist, year after year, in what she considers my neurotic persistence in hidebound Christian tradition. But she is kind and good and sweet; and she will inevitably say, "Well, we really worship the same God."

Nonsense. She believes, very slightly, in a home-made version of "universalist" Oriental mysticism, having neither the asceticism for Brahminism nor the commitment for Zen.

The same God? They don't even look alike. Hers is invisible, even to creation; my Lord is like fire, like gold and bronze. His hair is white as wool, his eyes glowed the sun into light, and he spoke the universe into being; he receives my death with sorrow for my suffering and with joy for my coming to him; he weeps when his sparrows fall, and he let his own Son cry "It is finished!" so that I could have his life in me. No cosmogony, no tragic matings of godlings, no grunting issue of earths and beings here: it's all created in his speaking.

Once I was just a high-school girl going to Sunday School and church, probably looking at pictures in wallets while the sermon passed over our heads in the choir loft. I knew about God, I knew the story of Jesus; but I didn't know the Christ, the Dancing One.

In those days, my mother was constantly bombarding with such axioms as "Be good, sweet maid, and let who will be clever."

Now, I'll never know just why my mother said that to me: pianist-poet-teacher, she is and was always clever. At any rate, as some of my friends tried to become Donna Reed types (perfect mothers and wives, who waxed their glassy floors in three-inch heels and woke up with lipstick on) and others went to be ethnologists in Trobriand, I became, lamentably, neither very good nor very clever.

I was a student and mother and piano teacher and very occasional poet, who at times produced brilliance and at other times gave up quickly or even destroyed my own success, either whimpering alone or lashing out at those who saw me fall. Because I never knew that to be clever might also be, for me, the best kind of being good.

We were told what to do, we women who grew up in the forties and fifties: we were to rebuild America, to be fruitful and multiply. Marriage, preferably to a GI Bill student, was the garden of Eden, where wives got a Ph.T. degree—a "putting hubby through" certificate—when our spouses graduated. If we got our own academic degrees, they were submerged in our womanhood. If we got Phi Beta Kappa keys, we laid them to rest in jewelry boxes where they opened no doors. We were gladly subsumed under our husbands' names.

And then we got a mortgage and kids and the PTA, and some of us were happy and some were miserable. But we wanted to do what was right, and we didn't know—some of us until we were grandmothers—that what was right is often what is desired in secret. We were like the prodigal son's older sister, waiting for our party, waiting for something, never having the nerve to tap our own inner resources until someone said, "Go for it!" and we found Christ.

I found him in stages, from my infancy through my adulthood; but when I really found him, all in one piece, it was too late for me to go to seminary; my bones ached too much to spend the rest of my life in some convent; and I was too bound by love for my children to run away with God, except within the secret of my heart.

"Ah only want to do what mah Laard calls me for," I heard a radio preacher say. "The hahd paht is knowin' his will."

No, the hahd paht is knowing that we can't really serve him. He doesn't really need us. He has the angels for his servants: us he wants for children. It isn't hard to know what God is calling us to do: it's usually what we like best. I know that, now.

But too often, someone like me goes wandering about through the labyrinths of life, rejecting her own more obvious gifts, while wondering what to become; and finally the Shepherd comes and gets that one, a ninety-ninth sheep, perverse and foolish. That trip home on his shoulder is pretty incredible, let me tell you.

Here in Oregon there are few shepherds any more: the sheep safely graze, as did Bach's sheep, but they do it in fenced pastures, not like those that are tended by humans even today in Bethlehem and Amman and the Loire Valley. Here they rest on green velvet knolls beside still waters where God's pure and holy light splinters fragment after fragment of diamond persuasion into rainbows and dancing points, all for the uninterrupted and unshared joy of sheepdom.

One summer, after we had left cement streets and come to Oregon, my son showed his prize goat at the state 4-H fair; and because she was a lonely goat who got depressed and grouchy at fairs, he slept at night in her pen in the huge sheep-and-goat barn of the fairgrounds. I woke at midnight in the mothers' dormitory and wandered out to check on them. And there he was, the Good Shepherd, fourteen years old, my third and youngest child, an only son, then too short for his age, sound asleep with his head on the goat's back and his arm thrown in careless love around her neck.

Her name was Alice, and she had yellow eyes with square pupils; his are green, green as glasswort; and they both opened their eyes and looked at me for a moment, unseeing; and then they went back to their blessed Sabbath, into that rest which we all may enter (if we listen, on a day called Today).

Now my son is in his late twenties and wears a lion's beard. His sister Susan, Andrew's mother, is tall and lovely, with her children and her sculpture and her flute; and his other sister, Carol, our Christ-mas-morning gift, has great grey eyes and is full of love. They are grown now, not much like the rosy babes I held in my lap.

But Andrew looks much like my son did at two years old: his cheeks are apricot and his hair is corn-colored, and his joy is complete.

I longed for joy when I was a confused, depressed young mother, struggling to clean the house that seemed to hover over me, hostile; sometimes I took college classes or gave piano lessons, but sometimes I did nothing at all. And sometimes I even tried to commit suicide. I was always looking for God, or rather, the Something More I kept hearing that God had for me. I looked in all kinds of places: grand, empty cathedrals and silent forests and dim corners; I read dusty books and went to meetings of vague people who said they had an Answer.

Therefore it was to my utter and complete astonishment that I found him, found my joy complete.

One day I was reading my Bible and idly thought, or prayed, "God, I want what it tells about here." Nothing happened, or rather, nothing happened that I could detect; but a few weeks later I found my joy complete in, of all places, a full church, with a badly-played organ, birthday pennies bouncing on the floor, and children shuffling restlessly.

He was *there*. There, in the same liturgy, in the same Prayer Book that I had been reading every Sunday morning for a million years, in the prayer read every week for purity ("Almighty God, unto whom all hearts are open, all desires known, and from whom no secrets are hid . . . cleanse the thoughts of our hearts by the inspiration of your Holy Spirit . . ."), he suddenly jumped out from between the rubrics, looked at me with Lion's eyes and said, "Let's dance!"

Andrew and I danced this afternoon, in the backyard, and I know Christ danced with us. Andrew likes to toss the last-year's nuts, lying on the ground, with abandon. Now Christ's eyes are like these hazelnuts: they glow, deep-colored, with the dance, with resurrection life, with himself. He cannot weep forever, you know; not even for our sins. Those shining eyes were meant for joy and redemption and judgment.

"After all," they say in Narnia, "He's not a tame Lion."

I wonder when Andrew will stop dancing with me. Now he is two, two and beautiful and wicked to his kindly parents; and he is willing to dance with me under the filbert trees, while I sing. How long will it be until he is horrified or embarrassed at the sight of his crazy grandmother dancing like a blond bear with Christ?

"Grannuther!" he cried, flinging an enormous hand-ful of nuts. "I think I saw Jesus dancing too!"

If he can look through me, past me, and see Christ forever, he'll know it's all right.

II
A FIELD WHERE PAN WAS SEEN

Jesus said to her, " . . . go to my brethren and say to them, I am ascending to my Father and your Father, to my God and your God." Mary Magdalene went and said to the disciples, "I have seen the Lord." (John 20:17,18)

Several years ago I crawled under a place of dusty brocade and candle wax to touch the stone that is over the stone of the Holy Sepulchre in Jerusalem. There, an Armenian Orthodox priest with a face like a tabby cat's, great whiskers jutting over his smooth round cheeks, and whose dancing, ancient eyes looked past me at Christ (constantly being entombed and resurrected in the pupil and cornea of an inner truth), sprinkled me with holy water, and gave me a small plastic crucifix labeled "Jerusalem."

In the second between kneeling to peep at the back of his tomb, and the shouting of the tour guide to move on, I managed a quick prayer for my own consecration, looking into the divine anarchy of that priest's amber eyes. For a moment we held each other in sight, and his veiled hat bobbed with mysterious emphasis, along with the grace of the holy water; and then I crawled out and asked the guide not to shout at us while we prayed.

We had come slowly, a group of us, taking turns carrying a heavy wooden cross up the Via Dolorosa. We knelt in the street at each station to proclaim that he had redeemed the world; and then we came to say the last three Stations of the Cross inside the church.

The church itself is the holiest kind of madness. Every architect born in a thousand years seems to have added to its shape; inside, a host of acolytes, choir boys, priests, and deacons nod, bow, genuflect, and sometimes stumble joyfully over each other, singing angelic responses in Greek, Armenian, Syriac, Latin, and whatever other esoteric and enchanted tongues worship may inspire.

There are altars everywhere, icons everywhere, silver and gold enough to pave heaven, and great cables that hang down at least fifty feet to bring light in glass-shaded oil lamps. As I watched all those priests celebrate, and choirs sing, and tourists, both reverent and otherwise, roam through the stretches of marble and porphyry and solid gold, an organ that I could never find began to play.

We searched and at last found some pipes, but no console or organist; yet loud and convincing, this grand instrument began to play Bach's "Sheep May Safely Graze."

Great glory! To think that Bach, one of the strongest and most lyrical voices of the Reformation, and forbidden by all Catholicism until after Vatican II, should stream forth like molten gold at the world's holiest, and most triumphant, shrine! It was like a confirmation of God's sovereignty.

Just as the music was apparently organless, so it was unrelated to any of the magnificent liturgies going on around us. It rose over voices, choirs, Sanctus bells, heights, depths, death, life, angels, powers, principalities, and the murmurs of tourists. In the cloud of incense that fills that ancient basilica with God's consuming and compelling glory, in the place where we saw a woman put a huge diamond ring on a statue of the

Lady of Sorrows, and where another knelt before a crucifix to place kiss after weeping kiss on the feet of Christ, I heard my favorite Bach pour forth as from the mouth of heaven.

Standing before the great altar, I began to hum, and so did a woman behind me; but I think she hummed another tune. Did we all hear the same melody? Or did someone else hear Mozart or Hindemith or the Beatles? I began to wonder if it were really Pentecost, the first Pentecost, the only Pentecost, and the organ just began to play itself in utter ecstasy at the presence of the Holy Spirit.

And the sheep that safely grazed in Bach's pasture, and in the Church of the Holy Sepulchre, are in his care, everywhere.

"We are the people of his pasture and the sheep of his hand," shouts the choir on Sunday mornings, in the *Jubilate Deo.*

Singing and grazing and dancing are fit pursuits for the people of his pasture. When, ten or so years ago, we kept a herd of goats on a small farm a hundred miles from here, the kids of those goats used to dance in the spring; and I knew how the ancients might have seen those baby goats dancing to a pre-incarnation theophany and might have called that vision "Pan."

C. S. Lewis said that such pagan things were "good dreams"; they were a way of God's sending us pictures, of remembering forward, to Christ.

Those ancients weren't sure, then, who the Person was; but baby goats, who are innocent, as all the beasts are innocent, knew who that was dancing with them in the pasture, with his Lion's eyes pleading that men and women, too, taste his kind of madness and make joy complete.

Young goats can stay on their hind legs for a long while; a Department of Agriculture Extension agent once told me that it was to strengthen them for high-reaching browsing in adulthood. But I know better. That kind of ecstasy is training to "own a Deity nigh," as the Christmas carol suggests.

We are the people of his pasture, you and I and Andrew and the beasts, safe to sing and graze and dance. And the next time I see a goat kid on its hind legs, I'll burn incense.

There was no incense at the Garden Tomb, where we went only an hour after our trip to the Church of the Sepulchre. This is Protestantism's claim to a shrine, also known as Gordon's Calvary. We were directed to go out and see, and were shown pictures of, a rock escarpment, a place where buses park, and I jumped to realize I was looking at a skull.

There in the rock were the grin and grimace of Death, the eyesockets empty, the nose a long, dark oval. Golgotha, Place of the Skull. To say the least, I sucked in my breath; and then we were pointed, through the beautiful garden with its red anemones and white primroses, to a tomb hewn in the cliff.

Only one side of what had been intended as a two-person mausoleum had ever been finished; perhaps it had been used for only a few hours. For some reason I looked up, and I saw a great sunburst of what I assumed to be iron oxide, leaping out in rays of yellow-gold on the ceiling. I pointed at it, and my husband and I were caught, caught, transfixed, by the pattern of what looked like a great explosion of light.

We sat in the tomb for a long time, not talking. There were no Masses, no choir boys, no organ: we sat in what was perhaps Revelation's half hour of silence in heaven. It might have been forever that we sat there, resting and thinking and praying. And then we suddenly got up, still not speaking, and went outside and looked at great flat stones and the carven tracks in which they roll. I wondered if angels left handprints, but found only well-worn Jerusalem granite.

It was Apart. Some things and some places, and even some people (like the monk at the sepulchre), are Apart. They are in tune with another system; perhaps their molecules move differently, hearing not a different drummer but a different Word, still resounding from the moment of creation; and the place of the garden tomb was one of these, Apart.

We saw people move through the garden, and we talked to them. Near the first-century winepress, a woman wearing a sari, with dark skin and a red dot on her forehead, said she was from Texas: I didn't stop to ask, but nodded and went on. Things there were possible.

When we came back to our own country, the pastor of my church asked me, "Well, which one did you believe was authentic? The Holy Sepulchre, or the Garden Tomb?"

Without hesitation, I answered, "I believe both of them are the place where Jesus was entombed."

"How can that be?" chimed in a listener.

"I understand," he said, laughing in a way that reminded me of Christ's gentle laugh, and he went to write his sermon. And I went to tell my sisters and brethren, "I have seen the Lord."

III
HUCKLEBERRY CHRIST

> John was dressed in a rough coat of camel's hair, with a leather belt round his waist, and he fed on locusts and wild honey. His proclamation ran: "After me comes one who is mightier than I. I am not fit to unfasten his shoes. I have baptized you with water; he will baptize you with the Holy Spirit." (Mark 1:6-8, NEB)

Recently I attended a workshop on liturgical dance. I came home tired, restless, disgruntled.

"What was so wrong?" my husband asked me.

"It was just too civilized," I said, reflecting on the long afternoon of self-conscious motion and spiritless dancing. "I don't think God is impressed by fancy manners."

Perhaps I come by these feelings honestly. I grew up near Indian reservations where I saw liturgies danced, and they weren't civilized; in fact, some of them shocked my sensibilities terribly. The reality is that liturgical dance, like anything that purports to be a response to God, can, at the primal level, seem sensual or barbaric or violent or even cruel; it can certainly wound one's sense of religious propriety. It is not an easy thing, for instance, to see a woman whipped so that she can become a full tribe member, nor to see a man forced to vomit during his puberty initiation. We see these things as savage, barbaric, not fit for modern men and women. But whoever asked us to be so decent and dainty?

Passion is always better than manners. My grandmother, in her sixties, was struck with whips in a tribal dance of liturgy. She had taught on the Navajo reservation for many years, and when she was invited to become a member of the People, she happily embraced the suffering that might accompany her acceptance into the tribe. Younger women, who loved her, ran in to take some of the whip cuts, but her own skin was seared and bleeding as she humbled herself for Love.

Now, I have been going to and fro in the earth and reading the Gospels and praying, and I know that I must indeed lose both my sanity and my civilization to become fit for God's company, because "civilization," as it is presented, is usually only a justification of passivity. We call it civilized to do what's *natural*, what comes easiest, and then we fence that natural act in with laws and mores and rites.

For instance, one of the arguments for capital punishment is usually couched in a question: "What would you do if someone broke in and tried to kill you? Shoot, or let them kill you?"

The natural answer is "Shoot." But then Christ keeps asking us to be more than natural, asking us for a second mile for foolishness, for a refusal to be part of the world around us even while trying to serve and save that world.

Civilization gave us territorial rights, the murder of Thomas á Becket, and charity that begins and ends at home. It promotes the belief that everyone on earth should be like us here in America, and suggests that progress really means technology. Civilization brought the guillotine, the nuclear bomb, racial segregation, and the X-rated movie.

"But what about penicillin, free public education, open heart surgery, and democracy?" cries John Stuart

Mill, who moves the elbow joint of my mighty right arm.

Granted. But the trouble, Millie, is that although your Utilitarian kind of civilization proclaims equal rights, it sets up an elite who decide what is best for everyone, what will give the most happiness to the most people. I think that the most dangerous person in the world is someone who knows what's best for anyone, and that the most dangerous doctrine in the world is one that holds "happiness" up as the ultimate goal of life.

Now, "society," which seems to be anything a writer decides it is, has proposed a kind of moral Laodicea for us all. The minds that prevail over this generation's society speak of love, and everyone hugs a lot; but society also preaches that divorce is probably the best—nay, the only—answer to marital strife, and that euthanasia or suicide are the specifics to relieve suffering. Nowadays we consider it civilized to speak decently, even affectionately, to one's former spouse at dinner parties, but grossly embarrassing to say passionately, at those same parties, that Christ is calling us.

But those on the professionally religious side of civilization, who rail at us about homosexuality and dirty movies and abortion and a lack of patriotism, may be missing the Big Sins of society. They wrap the cross in the national flag and suggest that God will punish us for our lusts and our disregard for national security. Might they end up at the gates of hell, crying "Lord, Lord," unheard because, like those whom Amos and Jeremiah and Jesus warned, they ignore the cries of the poor and the downtrodden?

But what of God's saints, his great ones? Did they avoid the ipecac or the lash?

"Purge me with hyssop!" cries the psalmist in unadorned praise, not afraid to injure our tender socialization nor to conjure up ugly images, because he was speaking intimately to the Most High. Saints usually seemed to ignore manners in favor of morality, and civilization in favor of true ceremony. Their nationalism was usually insignificant, and they thought propriety trivial unless it was part of charity. John Hus was God's fool when he trusted the "safe conduct" to Leipzig. Teresa of Avila drove people crazy with her outspoken criticism of the ruling class. Thomas More rejected the polity of the crown for the tumultuous truth of the cross. In thirty-nine years, nearly four thousand Quakers were killed, or died in prison, seeking spiritual truth even at the risk of being called traitors. Mother Teresa of Calcutta ignores the "me first" ethos of our time and would give her legs to lepers if she could. Gandhi was so out of touch with what the world teaches that rather than seeking revenge with his last breath, he made the Hindu sign of forgiveness as he fell under the assassin's gunshot. Martin Luther King, having been on the mountain, was like St. Paul, who, not really concerned about dying, made himself vulnerable to death.

In the face of all this humanity, I wonder why we think that it's necessary to make Christianity, at the level of church, of worship, so cold and distant, so socially correct. Manners are wonderful: they issue from the throne as a blessing to us so that we may live and worship with some predictability. But passionless manners, done for civilization's sake, are silly and maybe even wicked.

The life of Jesus on earth is dusty and dirty and sweaty; it is filled with what someone might call antisocial acts. God didn't suddenly transform a holy man into a heavenly being; he sent a man right from his own bosom, who ate and slept and sweated and died, died violently. And then when he had been in the grave long enough that his friends probably feared he was suffering what we delicately call "corruption," God raised him up—glorified, yes, but still as the first real human being.

Why can't we see what God has always told us? He is not content with history to tell us that Christ is the holy Wild Man. He makes sure that everything we read or sing or dance is full of the lonely heroism that affirms that "good dream" of desocialization in us; and the vision he gives may be, but is not necessarily, dressed in a hair shirt: a vision that is lifted up in rapture created by the deepest experience of God.

Literature is full of him. Look at Huck Finn, alone in the river's midst, poling his raft with the absolute current. Is there anyone more like the lonely Jesus, who went with what must be?

Listen to Huck. "I knowed it was wrong of me to let that nigger get away," he says in glorious indictment of humanity at its worst. Huck hates the world when he puts on its glasses, for there he encounters a Gospelline assortment of knaves and weaklings, politicians and Pharisees; there, also as in the Gospels, the most openly wicked are at least led by passion and a kind of wounded innocence, and the most politic are led by lust or avarice. From his raft's-eye view, Huck tells me that civilization, sophistry, and sorcery were never God's inventions: they came from humanity or the Enemy, or a conclave agreement of the two.

Yet Huck rejected the more obvious choices that the nineteenth century offered, staying to his Little Rule within a deeper romanticism. He keeps his discipline: when he and Tom Sawyer dig the runaway slave, Jim, out of jail as if they were pirates, they unchain the black man each night so that he can help them dig, and put him back in chains at daybreak.

A waste? Passion spent on a flower that might wilt? No, because they were doing it as pirates, in the manner of heroes. No, because if they, if we, eschew pirate lore or strophes of poetry or the sounds of harmony, if we abandon e. e. cummings and Goethe or Beethoven and Schumann for today's "reality," all we have left is the cadence of exploding bombs. And No, because if my heart be anything but a foolish instrument of God's praise, I might become the tinkling cymbal of the most uninspired kind of theology or the sounding brass of economic determinism.

How do I know the world is wrong? Because at the end of the *Huckleberry Finn* narrative, Huck tells those who would invite him into a warmer, safer world, "I got too much sense to get sivilized [*sic*] again."

I read *Huckleberry Finn* the first time when I was eight years old; I haven't yet read it for the last time. And all my life, in everything I read or sang or watched, from *The Book of Live Dolls* to *Catch-22* to *E.T.*, Jesus Christ kept popping up and saying, "This is the story of our adventure together. This is the road map. This is me."

Sometime in late youth I was caught up when Holden Caulfield, in Salinger's *Catcher in the Rye*, confesses and laments, "I'm the worst liar in the world; I really am." Here he betrays an innocent heart to the false world. It was really to Holden's credit that he tells the kind of lies he does: his fantasies reveal an outcry against the crude, cruel apathies of humankind.

Holden, like Christ, was most splendid when he was suffering. As he walked alone at midnight by the frozen duckpond in Central Park, despairing and lonely, he revealed the broken and agonized heart of One in Gethsemane, whose friends could not watch even an hour.

And in the case of both Christ and the Catcher, the only faithful believer seems to be a passionate girl. Ole Phoebe, Holden's sister, comes to the duckpond much as Mary of Magdalene peered into the Tomb. Ole Phoebe brings Holden the gift of her allowance; Mary brings spices to Christ. Both acts are uncivilized, stubborn, irrational. Why bring money to Holden, whose cause is already lost? Why bother to anoint a body three days dead in a hot climate?

Lack of decency, a grand loss of propriety, and the refusal to sit in a motionless mourning give action to wild and savage loves. We see both Phoebe and Mary, silhouetted in the light of our exploding munitions plants, shorn of dignity or reputation or consideration of consequence, wearing the linen garment of the Bride eager for her Groom. These two are pure products in a world of fakes and false mutations.

Not once did Jesus choose companions who were decent or civilized. As Huck chose Tom Sawyer, Jesus chose excitable Peter, whose strengths and weaknesses both lay in his passion. Tom Sawyer, too, lacked strength at times; but he was still uncivilized enough to dig Jim out of jail with a case knife. Jesus took a Zealot and an unlettered Galilean; Huck chose a fake duke and a runaway slave.

Huck Finn, Holden Caulfield, and Christ: as unlikely as it seems, I believe that all stories are one Story. *The Ugly Duckling, Dick Whittington, Sleeping Beauty,* and *Klods Hans* are all stories about heroes under an enchantment or strangely downtrodden, who wake or come home or somehow are transformed, resurrected, glorified. Thus when Jesus came to tabernacle among us, he deliberately took on customary enchantment by the world's wicked prince. Cleverly, our Father told us, over and over, in story and song, of how fallen humanity would be redeemed, how whoring Israel would be restored, how the sleeping woman would waken at the kiss of the True Prince; and then he made us gasp with amazement at the truth of the dead Jesus, resurrected into Christ the Victor King.

I think I suspected it all my life. I think I knew, deep down, that I was reading about resurrection when, like Siegfried, I found Brunhilde in the Ring of Fire. I knew it was Christ's redemption of the world I heard about in

Beauty and the Beast. And I knew who it was when my father read me Kipling's *Yellow Dog Dingo*, who ran on and on.

Suddenly, immediately, faster than the speed of society's sound, I am on the trail of Jesus the Wild Dog. On goes Dingo, yellow dog Dingo; on runs the Wild Dog, yellow Dingo-Jesus, transcending manners and magic, running over the earth with his chest high enough for spears or guns, running and dancing over the face of this planet in the same way that lightning tears up the atmosphere. There is no real choice: as the song of the sixties said, I want to follow with him, I want to follow blind. I want to follow blind, all right: he is irresistible!

Following blind is a risky business. Grace is chancy at first look. Ski jumps, falling in love, climbing trees, praying—all risky. If I go out on a limb, will someone laugh at me? If I jump off a sand dune in a hang-glider, will I melt over the sea, like Icarus? If I walk on the water of the sea, will I beach like a crazed whale and die in a cloud of sand fleas, with deep groans of agony and despair? What if I stand before the throne of God, unworthy, ritually unpurified: will I die? Would it be safer to hang the Fleece on a golden nail in the temple, or throw it back in the sea and chase it?

Following blind is child's play, child's loving. Andrew is nearly three now; and one night before Easter, we let him stay up to see the Narnia film on television. Afterward, a well-known five-part movie about Jesus was running.

Andrew was toddling down the hall in his sleepers after the cartoon, and I asked the roomful of people, "Does anyone want me to leave the TV on to see Jesus?"

Andrew ran back to the den, his eyes wide and glistening with the love of God.

"Jesus?" he crowed. "On TV? Oh, *yeth*, Grannuther, I want to see him!"

Andrew, my love, so do I. But we'll have to look for him where things and people are running free. The ultimate of civilization, of security, is a prison, where one would not need to make any decisions about food or clothing or activity, or take the risk of thinking or becoming something. But a bird on a bush, albeit wild, is also secure, not because of the bush but because of its wings.

Therefore, I will no longer be conformed to this world, but transformed by a renewal of my mind. I shed the world's kind of civilization like another year's skin; I have to give up its manners to learn the courtesy of Christ; I must risk everything and go to the store and the bank and the church and friends' houses, carrying that most barbaric and loathsome of sights, Christ's broken body.

I must go where Dingo goes, where Huck Finn goes. I must not put Christ in a petting zoo, as a tame God whom I can visit at will: for to follow Christ is to track the wild dog to the suburbs of madness, to the back of the cave, to the outer ring of the planet, pursuing him as I might seek the source of an elusive sound in the night.

Recently I woke to such a sound. At first my mind (preferring deep sleep) said, "It is the dogs, untimely wanting out of the garage."

But certain qualities made those sounds seem the result of human action: I heard a drawer being opened, a chair scraping, something being wound up.

Too sleepy to have good sense and waken my husband, I went barefoot into the living room. There, at 4 A.M., was Justin, my neighbor's three-year-old son, who sometimes plays with Andrew. He had wakened, felt bored, and wandered into my house, which was, for some reason, unlocked that night. When I found him, he was playing with toys that he knows I keep in a cherrywood chest for grandsons and other honored

guests. He was also eating my fresh-baked choco-
late-chip cookies, this Justin, clad in a pajama top, wet
cotton training pants, and a pair of huge rainboots.

There he was: Christ the Child, the Wild God, the
Vital Innocent. He was the pursued pursuer, playing on
my living-room floor as if he had a perfect right to be
there.

How did I dare walk out there unprotected? What if
it had been a thief or a rapist? Would that have been
Christ, too? If I had a last memory of beady black eyes
and hot dirty breath and physical pain, would I have
awakened later, and found myself in Christ's arms?

Worse could have happened.

"Worse than rape or death?" cries the Survivalist fig-
ure in the painted totem pole of my reason.

O yes, yes, much worse, little tin soldier. Much worse
than any of those things. For to be the offender is far
worse than being the victim. What if, instead of looking
at the child who sat there, I had walked out, certain of
my rights, closed my eyes, and pulled a trigger? Would
that destroyed, innocent breast have bled onto wild yellow fur? In trying to stanch bleeding, might I have had
to tear away a Raftsman's shirt? Could I have shot an
intruder and discovered that I had killed God?

I cannot enter the presence of God carrying any
weapon that the world provides. Society offers me guns
and keys and locks; it offers certainty and righteousness; it holds out the worst kind of sorcery and blasphemy, predicated on the proposition that it's every
man or woman for himself or herself.

Well, every man or woman *is* for Himself, and don't
you forget it. We are for Christ, to be dug out with a case
knife, if necessary, as his drama of salvation is enacted.

Jesus Christ never protected himself from violence by
violence of his own. When it came down to his life, he
didn't protect himself at all, and we cannot protect ourselves, civilize ourselves, and still be his. It's a risky

business, this following Jesus blind. What was Ole Phoebe doing, looking for someone she loved in Central Park at midnight, anyhow? What made Mary Magdalene think she could roll that huge stone away, even if she didn't get assaulted by a drunken guard? Why wasn't Huck Finn in a good foster home? Why didn't I have enough sense to take a gun into my living room when I heard a noise?

Because God is good. I thank him that I do not take a gun in pursuit of sound, nor in pursuit of Jesus the Wild Man. Because once having glimpsed him, I got too much sense to get sivilized again.

Gimme a case knife, Tom.

IV
SETTING THE CAPTIVES FREE

The Spirit of the Lord is upon me, because he has anointed me to preach good news to the poor. He has sent me to proclaim release to the captives and recovering of sight to the blind, to set at liberty those who are oppressed, to proclaim the acceptable year of the Lord. (Luke 4:18-19; cf. Isaiah 61:1-2)

Martha pushes hard on this Tuesday morning: there is much to be done. My neighbors and I are planning a garage sale for the coming weekend, because the fruits of our labors are piled high. This year's harvest of household junk was great, and our storehouses are too full.

There is much to prepare, but my Mary muse wants this writing hour, even though Martha says, "There's too much work; besides, that desk looks like a shipwreck."

At the garage sale we will sell until sold out. Evangelists like to say, "I'm sold out for Jesus!" and I love the sound of that; but as I write these words, I do it on a very expensive word processor, equipment I worked hard to afford.

C. S. Lewis hated typewriters and wrote every elegant and inspired word of his books and his stories in a methodical copperplate. One time I tried writing by

hand for a whole day because sometimes I like to pre-
tend I am Lewis or John Donne or someone lone and
ascetic and slothless. All I got for my day's effort was a
tired wrist and a few pages of illegible uphill scrawl in a
crabbed hand.

"Are all apostles? all ascetics?" whispers the St. Paul
digital recording, revolving just above my hippocam-
pus. No, dear Saint. I know, I know. The message is
always different for each of us. After my day of writing
I went back to my word processor; and until I get rid of
it, and my wonderful electric blanket, get rid of a food
processor that can make peanut butter faster than I can
open a jar, and a Japanese piano that would make Bach
cry out with delight, I guess I am not "sold out" for
Jesus.

Unless by "sold out" one means that everything in
my "real" life tends to be an interruption of prayer and
an intrusion into my sweet conversation with Jesus.
That part is true; in fact, sometimes I feel frivolous about
the world around me because God in his heaven seems
so much denser, so much more real, than this: thick and
solid is the supernatural, compared to this ephemeral
day.

Most of the neighbors who are participating in the
garage sale have no idea that I am a crazy lady who
dances for joy with the Lord, whether under the filbert
trees or in the slow dance of the Eucharist. They have
seen me, the neighbors have, entering my car with my
Prayer Book or Bible, perhaps oftener than they deem
necessary: they think I am "churchy," but probably
harmless. They are willing to excuse my excessive love
for Christ because they have met me in clothing stores
and at Tupperware parties and neighborhood events,
and because they have heard me swear when I tripped
over my two useless white Maltese dogs.

They could probably cope with the fact that I *am*
sometimes caught to rights reading theology or sitting

in silent meditation. After all, even pro tennis players meditate. But I wonder if they will be ill at ease, say, at the next baby shower, if they read this and find out that I make trips into the woods with Jesus, where we break bread, and I eat it and he glows among the violets and oxalis, like a streaming sun. Can they cope with the idea that I am stilled and quieted out there where ferns renew their vows to him, vows of obedience, as he sings the afternoon into being? Will all this make them squirm and drop their eyes and twist their festive paper napkins?

Ah, this is the dangerous life, this Christianity. As Annie Dillard says in *Holy the Firm*, "It becomes clear we are dealing with a maniac." He is a completely mad God, a fiery ball of love, sweeping the galaxies with that compelling love, and forcing them (by grace) to the dance.

The biggest risk lies in the fact that once loved by him, we can become like him, constrained to constant motion by the burgeoning abundance of his love. We are empowered in his divinity, priested by Christ's priesthood, royal in his kingdom: and our prayers turn to fire.

Once I saw a horrifying television commercial where "onion breath" became visible as a dark green balloon issuing from the offender's mouth. Mercy! A fearsome sight: but what an idea! For if we could see our prayers, see the forms they take and the colors they wear, those prayers closest to the Father's will would be fires. We storm the gates of hell with fierce, hot prayers, and those gates cannot prevail against us. Our lips send forth great tongues of fire at the gates, and at those gates I plead no mercy: captives are in those cells.

Last Saturday I saw one of the captives at the hospital. She is emerging, like a wriggling thing, from a cottony pupa, from deep depression, from that long and vast and dark sorrow that regularly, periodically, thrusts itself into her, intruding like granite until she stares at the floor and cannot see the heaven beyond her darkness.

She has a kind, confounded young husband who does not understand that the lithium carbonate, which magically brought her eyes into focus, came to her lips from the Lord's chalice. (All miracles are his miracles: what are they arguing about, out there in the wastelands?)

Saturday, her eyes were still wide and sad and touched with the remainder of her great psychotic sadness. Poor bird, with her lovely short hair in greasy feathers; but as we talked, she began to push her bangs off her forehead and speak of having a bubble bath: Jesus leapt clear to the ceiling of the visitors' room, and twelve thousand angels cried "Holy!" because a captive was being set free.

Sunday, I was the church chalice-bearer, and as I was concentrating on the stately quadrille of Eucharist, I bent over a bowed head, lifted the chalice to trembling lips, and saw that it was she kneeling there. The hospital had released her for a few hours for church, and she sat and knelt quietly while her freshly-showered body and clean amber hair glowed like coals in the hot light of the fires of our prayers.

Her doctor calls her illness "affective disorder," which is a new name for manic-depressive psychosis. Some of her friends think she needs counseling and some that her problem is chemical; one woman even went to the hospital and tried to exorcise her from demonic possession.

No matter: the woman was foolish and spooky, to behave that way with a sick person, but any captive is a captive of hell until the gates are battered down. We storm the Enemy's citadel with our hot prayers; and as she emerges, tattered and wounded, from hell's terrible, sober sanity and begins to embrace the mad joy of the kingdom, Jesus dances and leaps high in his pleasure. My daughter, go in peace.

"Fires to the gates of hell? Isn't that like carrying coal to Newcastle?" asks Froggy the Gremlin, who lurks iconoclastically at my right hand. Ah, poor, sane, right-handed Froggy. The left hand is the dreamer: out of the left hand are the miracles worked and written, the treacle wells and warm oil of God's deliberate and joyful madness.

No, Froggy, hell is not a hot kingdom. Perhaps on the Day, God's final Day, there will be that terrible lake of fire to throw Death and Hades into. But that is God's fire, a different fire.

No, I think it's cold in hell, sane in there, dank and alone and seeping. Down there beyond all gracious acts and words, in that place of dark cisterns with unseen carven marble columns and lifeless stretches of black water, it's cold. Down there, below heaven's life, out of reach of the hot, glorious live spring where we can at least drink living water (even if we haven't yet met the Lion, the Lord of the Dance), down beneath the interchange of human song and motion, is the coldness, the uncomplicated thought, the terrible and defeating dishonesty that fixes itself parasitically in the gut and consumes all divinity that was breathed into us. And if the divinity is gone, all that is left is ourselves.

Now, if one goes to the same place frequently enough, one can become almost invisible. I go to hospitals and rest homes a lot, and doctors and nurses sometimes forget I am there and talk in front of me. One day a psychiatrist spoke to a rest-home nurse of an old, mad lady; and he asked, "Do you think there is any ego at all left in there?"

As they say in confession magazines, my heart sank. It sank. I could feel it slipping off the edge of the lifeboat and into the cold, sane, salty waters of the world's wisdom, and certain death. The heart chokes; it gasps for breath, pleads shrieking for life—and is instead weighted with carnal wisdom and pushed off into the icy, hellish, lifeless sea where murder is called mercy.

Is there any ego left, indeed! It is the fire of Divinity we want to see, not another dose of self. God asks his angels, "Is there any ego left in there?" and they hurt themselves at his heart. He asks us, his people, "Is there any ego left?" and we answer from a thousand positions and sizes and distances.

I for one am truly tired of writers and speakers who want to add to my already-dangerous ego by telling me that Jesus presupposes my self-love when he says, "Love your neighbor as yourself." They point out, nonempirically, that I cannot love others until I do love myself, that I cannot love him until I love myself, and that this Scripture—this summary of the Law and the Prophets—is nothing more than a simple lesson in self esteem.

Hogwash. When I was a tired, lonely, suicide girl, what kept me alive and out of the Pit was not self-love or self-actualization or identity or any of the thousand other popular terms for ego-indulgence. What kept me alive through a very long, unhappy first marriage, and divorce, and singleness at forty-one, and, finally, the blessing of the Church on a better marriage, what kept me from trying one more time to kill myself, after I emerged from one last, long, overdose-caused coma that should (by all rights) have killed me, what kept me alive through grey springtimes and wet autumns and hard winters was the fact that Jesus loved me, and that I found it impossible not to love him. I didn't have to love myself: he did it for me.

Recently my husband and my daughter Susan and Andrew went to the Anglican version of the old-fashioned camp meeting; and on the weekend, my son-in-law came too. There, in the lilac-laden breeze near one of Oregon's lovely small lakes, we gathered self-consciously under a canvas roof, our chairs mired in sawdust, to sing and study and pray for five days. Andrew dug in the sawdust and let the preaching and singing cover him like a canopy as he filled his yellow bucket and occasionally sprinkled it all over me.

The usual paradoxes prevailed: we spoke of a holy life —and ate enough food for a Third-World country to survive a month or more. We based a Bible study on the text that the Son of Man had nowhere to lay his head— and slept at night on urethane foam in self-contained trailers. And we indulged our egos in prayer.

Finally, at one of the evening services the guest preacher told us that we must indeed love ourselves before we even begin to love Jesus; and then we sang a song about becoming nothin', nothin' but the Spirit blowin' through us.

Well, I can hardly balance having love for myself on the one hand and becoming nothing but a vessel for the Spirit on the other; but before my restlessness dissolved into a devil's brew of impatience and theological superiority, one of the Coleman lanterns that hung on a rafter went out.

No one really listened to the sermon that the preacher kept on with; we were all watching someone who stopped to refuel the lantern and (since in that process, a mantle was broken) put on a new mantle. This lantern-play went on a foot or so away from me and suddenly! the light was bright and back on its rafter nail.

But then we were constrained to look again, and think, and murmur; then we all nodded, companions in the faith: because mantles burn on their own for awhile, sending up a putrid yellow flame that doesn't give much light or heat or inspiration at first. But when that skin had burnt off on our tent lantern, the holy ash that was left began to glow and hiss like a singing evening

star. Nothing, nothing left but the Spirit blowin'
through.

God, burn me off! Let me pulse and shine with that
delicate wick of ash: let my light so shine; let me be as a
lamp set on a hill. Consume my dross and refine my
gold, O God, until I am as pure as Thou: not only with
prayers of fire, but as fire all over.

So today at the rest home I look into filmed eyes, the
relentlessly writhing and chewing lips, the rocking
lower plate, the harsh, dark breath, the cataracts and
skin cancers, the thin and thinning hair that never
crowned nor was ever glorious; I look through the wak-
ing snore, the rasping chest, the clutching, sickly-white
hands, and do I ask, Is there any Ego left? Oh, no.

Letting fiery prayer continue to lick the gates of hell
and old age, I ask, "Is there any God left in there? Do
you still burn in there, you Jesus, you consuming fire?
Is the outpouring of your Holy Spirit still going on
behind that whitened, hooded eye?"

"I will not, will not, will not leave them; I will never,
no, never, no, never forsake them," he replies, eager,
impatient to get on with the important part: the Dance,
the Resurrection Dance.

V
DOWNTOWN CRAZY DAYS

Martha said to Jesus, "Lord, if you had been here, my brother would not have died. And even now I know that whatever you ask from God, God will give you." Jesus said to her, "Your brother will rise again." Martha said to him, "I know that he will rise again in the resurrection at the last day." Jesus said to her, "I am the resurrection and the life; he who believes in me, though he die, yet shall he live, and whoever lives and believes in me shall never die. Do you believe this?" She said to him, "Yes, Lord; I believe that you are the Christ, the Son of God, he who is coming into the world." (John 11:21-27)

On my way home from shopping, Jesus whispered to me that the supreme joke in all this Mary/Martha dilemma is that Martha is still dominating my life no matter how creative I become, because Mary would never write a book, any book, no matter how mystical it was. My cook, my housekeeper, is Martha (and I always visualize that part of myself waddling around among the convolutions of my brain, like a self-important goose in a ruffled dusting cap); and now I know that so is the self who sits in front of the word processor writing this book.

"But who is Mary, then?" I pled.

"She's that foolish woman who keeps a goat in her backyard for no reason, and makes nonsense sounds as her grandsons climb all over her," Jesus reminded me. "Mary is forever receiving, forever listening."

It's safest to be a Martha/doer, especially if what you're doing is his. It's the Mary life that takes all the risks. Mary's way, the listening way, takes all of me, shreds me inside. It's easiest when I am least aware: sometimes I waken at night, with the phrases of my listening held at almost-consciousness, just the way I sometimes wake with my finger holding the place in my book where I fell asleep.

Listening is complicated. It means I must quit praying and Pray, focusing everything on him, because listening isn't musing privately while the sermon goes on; one cannot listen and think at the same time, any more than one can catch all the voices in a recorded fugue while reading a book.

Mary the Listener can't hear anything but Christ: she can't hear the snarls of the Enemy, she shuts out the sounds of the freeway and the dishwasher and the television set and the background music in the dentist's office and the bank and the grocery store, music where it's always 1938 and the cocktail hour, where Ginger and Fred, in satins and tails, perpetually shake a chrome martini jar, their heads bobbing to the rhythm, like dolls.

(Background music must be doing at least as much to hide the face of God as do drugs or war. It is so much a part of modern life that when I came home today, I wondered what strange deliciousness surrounded me; and then I realized that it was silence, the silence in which heavenly music, always foreground, calls us and the Dance goes on.)

"But who dances? Martha, or Mary?" I asked. "Martha always seemed a little hidebound to me, too rational to be any kind of a dancer."

"Don't malign Martha," Jesus said a little sharply, as I congratulated myself on having a Mary consciousness for a moment. "I love her, you know. John wrote in his Gospel, 'Now Jesus loved Martha and her sister and Lazarus.'"

"I thought you liked Mary best," I told him.

"I said she had the better part, that day when Martha was being a compulsive hostess. And Mary was the one who broke the nard on my head and washed my feet in her tears. But look at what you yourself wrote down at the top of this chapter. It was Martha who called me the Son of God."

"But I thought—" I began, and then listened some more.

"It's the same kind of lie my enemies like to tell about Thomas. He said he couldn't believe without seeing, so I came where he could see me."

"But weren't you angry? I thought you implied that he should have believed the other disciples anyhow," I said.

"Judge not," he said, with his own exquisite brevity. "Besides, if it's so unspiritual to want to see evidence, why do you keep your eye fixed on the Bread when it's raised before Communion? Why is yours the one head in the whole congregation that always snaps up?"

"It's an opportunity for worship," I answered glibly.

"It was for Thomas too. I wasn't angry at him. I'm always happy when someone wants to see me. I told him, and John wrote it down in the twentieth chapter of his Gospel, 'Put your finger here, and see my hands; and put out your hand, and place it in my side; do not be faithless, but believing.' I'll do whatever it takes to help keep someone from being faithless, help them believe in me."

"Oh," I said, revising some things.

"You said in the first chapter of this very book that you always intend to worship me as Thomas did. Which of my other disciples said, 'My Lord and my God!'? Only Thomas. What other woman besides Martha said, 'I believe that you are the Christ, the Son of God, he who is coming into the world'?"

And he stole away, as quickly as a thief in the night.

"Oh," I said again, holding my mind open where he had been standing, as one waits in a doorway, watching a guest drive away; and after I had been still for a while, I unloaded the bags of plunder I had brought home from shopping.

There were a lot of people and things tripping and taunting the Dancers today. It was Downtown Crazy Days today, and the appellation was terribly wrong; for it was actually World's-Standards Sane Days today. Tight-lipped, suspicious salespeople in clown suits watched for shoplifters, and tired cashiers in pitifully drooping bird costumes were exhausted by the outdoor checkout lines, the pulling, the scrabbling.

A woman cut in front of me in the parking lot and then swore at me in her rear-view mirror as my brakes squeaked: I felt humanity rise up like acid in my esophagus. But then Christ, the High Priest, Emmanuel, the Lion of Judah and the Lord of the Dance, murmured, "Poor lady! Can't dance at all yet!" and asked me to pray for her. She looked angry and florid as she pulled into what I thought was my parking place, and she locked her car carefully before she hurried to the outdoor display of garden hoses.

Children were screaming and running in place while their mothers and their mothers' friends dug through bins of knit shirts and thong sandals. I saw one ochre-faced grandmother spurting cigarette smoke like a spouting whale, as she admonished a moaning little girl again and again to shut up and stand still. Willy-nilly, I began to moan and run in place, too: but I stopped for fear she would shake her finger and spit smoke at me too.

I heard one frizzle-haired woman snarl, "F'Chrissake, Harry, come on," tugging him into a shoe store. For Christ's sake, yes: he should have been going with her, leaping, waltzing with her like a roebuck, not playing a husband-wife tug-of-war, wits and winning, a game of Aces-spades-and-guess-who-will-be-boss-today. For Christ's sake, he should have been Jesus to his wife, offering her a heaven-sent smile and a cup of living water.

For Christ's sake, we should love one another not only as ourselves (which isn't much to ask) but as Christ loves us (which is everything). He loves his Bride, the Church, even as he cajoles her along, pleading for a little crippled love, sighing for her obedience. Never has he smote her with a fist or broken her heart; never has he abandoned her to go on welfare and raise the kids alone, nor has he ever sat, incommunicado, grunting and inscrutable in front of a television screen.

I was at a party once when a man I didn't know turned to me for no reason that I could discern and asked me, "What's the matter with American women?"

Without spilling a drop of my precious irony, I said, "American men," and delicately walked away, applauding myself. I had no business being so glib: that was before I myself truly took Christ's message radically. But glib or no, there was some truth to all that, y'know. Men have abdicated their love and let us forget our place.

"Our place?" cries the Barbie doll that hangs on the seam of my jeans, twirling her copy of the newly-proposed second ERA. "Our place, like being barefoot and pregnant, cooking on a wood stove?"

No, silly plastic woman. You know perfectly well that isn't what I'm talking about. I mean, men started treating us like commodities, so we got mad and forgot our place in the kingdom, as daughters. We should resist the temptation to let men think for us, but we should remember our royal heritage. And theirs.

"Why blame it on men?" asks Jesus, suddenly there again, his eye fixed on a half-dead piggyback plant on my bookshelf. "I never said you were supposed to get your identity from them. I told everyone to get it from me."

"Well, but Paul—"

Jesus wept.

"I'm sorry," I said. "I'm a fool, you know."

"I know," he said. "Let's dance."

"I have to water my plant," I said, beginning to feel better.

"Whose plant?" he cried, laughing; and I found that I was laughing now too, laughing aloud near an open window where the sound made my two backyard ducks rise and flap and quack in alarm.

I was instantly reminded of a day, years ago, when I stood on the beach facing the waves and sang "O Thou That Tellest Good Tidings to Zion," from *The Messiah*, to whatever or whoever wanted to listen. In those days I loved a young man who didn't like classical music and didn't exactly want to hear me sing it; but he sat very quietly, intrigued, because every time I came to "Arise!" with its little baroque trill, two brown seagulls at the vanguard of a flock of white ones would rise on tiptoe, flap their wings, and then settle down and wait for the next verse.

Anyone who has spent a day on the beach can usually see that gulls, like other creatures, are in joyful submission to their Father, who, another famous Seagull notwithstanding, is not the Big Seagull. Seagulls even sit in an order. And their Father, my Father, makes his face to shine upon us and them because he loves us, not because we have learned some cleverly immutable spiritual law.

But people, even people who are natural Marys (that is, who are by structure receptive, mystic, apparently born on the Ying side of things), are not always naturally obedient, as are seagulls and kangaroos and forest snails. Unless directed, even natural mystics sometimes point their listening only inward, believing that "finding" God and one's part in creation is a remembering process, like finally finding your socks after you've moved.

I have frustrating conversations with a friend who likes to "manifest" things. She tries to manifest a raise on her job or the end of an illness by aligning herself with what she believes are the laws of the universe. Then the cool God-mind within her knows whether or not these orders, or requests, are phrased in what she calls the "language of cosmic wholeness"; and Mind, as she calls her/him or it, reacts mindlessly, rather than granting or denying; and the reaction is positive toward her request according to how well she has used this language.

Good grief! A God like that can give no blessing. Only God's transcendence assures us of God's mercy. God is indeed within us; but if he is only within us, then God is completely subject to the confines and constraints of our own minds, and he would have no life outside his creation.

I once heard John Westerhoff, a priest and professor and writer, say at a conference that where there is no vision, there is no risk; where there is no risk, there is no witness; where there is no witness, there is no Gospel. I might add that where there is no Gospel, might there not also be no grace? The risk-free immanent-only God seems to me to be too limited, *is* creation (rather than its being his creature), adored only by inner pantheism where one regards one's own soul and tries to manipulate the universe like a string-jerked puppet.

No! "Holy! Holy!" the angels cry out, not to creation but to the creator, whose resurrected body now fills the universe (but by his knowing choice), to the Lamb slain before all worlds, to the Father whose majesty is greater than any of his created sunsets or tides or galactic motion. That Spirit whose will proceeds directly from the center of the Godhead certainly does not totally reside in anything created, even though I once heard a minister of a new-thought denomination announce that the title of his Christmas sermon would be "God Is a Mud Turtle."

If God resides only within us, then they will have to keep the human race alive forever lest God die indeed—not on the cross, but of emphysema or peritonitis or stomach cancer, spewing his last manifestation into a kidney basin.

But my gnostic friend who calls God "Mind" isn't the only type who tries (unknowingly) to exercise magic or witchcraft or manipulation of God by Praying Right. It isn't being done only by people in some cult. Some of my "really Christian" brothers and sisters are just as heretical, although they would cringe at that thought.

These advise us to use the prayer of faith in a way that turns belief into works, as neatly as a lathe turns wood. If we aren't healed, we don't pray right, or those who pray for us don't have enough faith. See, if you can just get a real handle on the Words of Prayer, then you've got God by the short hairs.

These people jerk Scripture up out of its setting like MacDuff from his mother's womb untimely ripp'd; then they shout them at me and God like alchemists intoning the formula for lead-into-gold: Believe in Your Heart and Confess with Your Mouth (and claim your miracle); Thank Him First (and he'll grant you anything); When Things Go Badly, Praise Him for It (and you'll get rich and well and have naturally curly hair). Good heavens! Have they forgotten that they speak of one whose Body is so holy that liturgicals even hold a silver dish beneath our chins at Communion, to catch the crumbs?

"Then why ask at all?" says the wooly-faced monk who has set up an altar behind my sternum. "Go to him in love only."

O dear anchorite, if only we could ask God for nothing but that he let us adore him! This is the kind of thought that holds me transfixed sometimes for hours and days at a time, so that on some days, when I open my heart to speak to him, words are not necessary, petition is not required. On those days I am content with being in his presence.

But on other days, ruled by my more rational side, worldly, constrained by love for someone else, troubled by myself, or stuck in a problem, I do ask. And I know that it does indeed have to be a prayer uttered in as much faith as I can muster; I do have to believe in my heart and confess with my mouth, because a relationship with him in which there were no trust would also bear no burden of love.

Therefore this schizophrenic, Mary/Martha debate rages endlessly, both within and without. Half of me is a contemplative, the other half stripped for action. Some days I want to be a medical missionary, nursing among lepers or teaching poor children with learning disabilities; other days, I want to dissolve into my own state of prayer. (And this says nothing about the days when I want to do neither, when I cry to the hills, "Fall on me!" in an attempt to hide from him.)

And I find in the world outside myself the same debate with heretical extremes as I note in my own nature. Half my argument is with those who believe that all they have to do is "manifest" what they know is already theirs: they say they have the same nature as God but have, because of sojourn in the world, forgotten how to get at it. For them, salvation consists of remembering how to be part of the divinity in which they automatically participate by virtue of being born. And the other half of the debate is with Christians who treat God as if he were a fool.

Is his power contained in a silicon chip, so that all we need to do is press the right word- or thought- or prayer-button for a printout? Or is he so stupid that he doesn't know what I mean when I falter in my words of prayer, or when my faith is thin? If that be true, there has to be a heavenly order book on a table by the throne, a book in which our prayers are recorded, according to how correct, how cunningly wrought they are.

Can you see it? The Father and the Son look over the orders. "Look here, Son. John Doe asked that his wife be healed of cancer; but he didn't praise me for her sickness, and he added 'But thy will be done, Lord.' Probably no faith at all. Let's kill her."

O awful shudder! My heart parts like the Red Sea, but armies wearing hobnailed boots tramp over the wet sand. No, no, no! No fool on the throne, no cruel test of prayer, no heavenly knee jerk.

Yet somewhere in the midst of all this prayer talk and these faith seminars there is truth. As I play a fugue, somewhere between my right and left hands there is a crossing of my thumbs and the right striking of a note. Somewhere in the midst of chaos, order emerges, the world grows round, the lights turn on, and God says, "Good." Somewhere, even in heresy, there is a beginning truth that needs to be snatched and run with toward the real goal. Because just as I chalk off some religious nonsense, God shows me that he is on the throne, running things.

We went to a dinner one night where an evangelist with a healing ministry was the speaker. I loved him on sight: he had gleaming short china teeth, dyed raven-black hair, and pink cheeks. Sweat rolled off his forehead as he spoke earnestly about salvation and healing of the body.

"He is able to deliver thee," he recited. "By his stripes we *are* healed. Rise up and walk. God will undertake to help his people."

I adored it. I wanted to look on the back of his neck and see if he had a Chatty ring to pull and produce these sweet, recorded sayings. He's a doll, I thought joyfully, a Plastic Preacher Doll.

And then I stood behind one of my sisters in Christ as he prayed for her healing. Great furrows of suffering and intercessory grief lined his pink brow, and I saw him cry with kindness when some of the broken and abused and imprisoned walked up or were wheeled up for healing prayer. He wasn't a doll: he was a man, a man imbued by the grace of another Man's love from the cross; and as I looked at him and his ministry, which is certainly not my liturgical style, I asked God to give me a flesh-and-blood heart instead of a stone heart.

That preacher believed. He laid his hands on people and believed, and the cherubim and seraphim put their wings over their faces and cried, "Holy!"

Then what of those on the other side, the side of tradition and conservatism? The right?

"Right?" shouts Mighty Mouse, emerging, fists raised, from my sock-top. "The right we fight for?"

No, Mighty, with your starry eyes. The right of left; those who are addicted to old wine. Like the minister who came to my bedside when my recurrent back problem flared up several years ago. He anointed me with oil and prayed for my healing; but when we talked afterwards, he confessed to me that this was for him not more than a sacramental act.

"What news, Father? Good news?" "Nay, daughter; no news at all." The man knew that I believe that God can make sick people well and turn water to wine and death to life and grief to joy and madness to holiness. He anointed me more on my faith than on his. What a grief, what a death, what a sorrow! No vision, no risk; no risk, no witness; no witness, no Gospel. No grace.

Mary, Martha; right, left; transcendent, immanent. The biggest risk of all is not knowing, is living with the paradox.

"Let's risk everything!" I cried to my dogs, and to Andrew, whose parents had loaned him to me for an hour. So we ran outdoors and let the goat out of her pen. She immediately ate the blooms on my yucca plant and chased a duck around the yard. Then she tried to stand on my knees as I sat on the steps of the deck.

"Get off, you dumb ruminant," I shouted, and the ducks quacked antiphonally. The goat put her warm, furry, sniffing nose against my cheek and stood there dreaming, swaying a little. Andrew climbed atop a pile of logs and, with a plant stake, conducted an unseen orchestra.

"O ye cattle, and ye beasts that creep upon the earth, bless ye the Lord, praise and magnify him forever!" I sang. The dogs barked as my husband came through the house and onto the back deck.

"What's going on out here?" he grinned, as the goat did a joyful one-and-a-half capriccio in the air for him, and Andrew shouted, "Gampa!"

"Crazy Days," I said, winking my mind's eye at Jesus, completely happy for the first time all day.

VI
THE BOUNDARIES OF HOLINESS

. . . whoever touches them shall become holy.
(Leviticus 6:18)

So Sarah laughed to herself, saying, "After I have
grown old, and my husband is old, shall I have
pleasure?" The LORD said to Abraham, "Why did
Sarah laugh?" (Genesis 18:12-13)

A time of tension is come. Cool rainy days have left my
arthritic bones aching. I was hurt by a friend, and I
filled my mouth with bitterness. A raccoon killed one
of our backyard ducks and ate the eggs from the nest of
another, and my husband and I used the occasion to
quarrel. It has been a time generally lacking in
holiness.

But I do know holiness when I see it.

Once I met a woman who could not move any part of
her body but her index finger and her lips. She could
not even speak in a normal voice, yet she spent her life
as a prayer counselor and suicide preventer. She could
answer her telephone by pushing a button and then
speaking in a hoarse whisper to the mouthpiece that
was taped to her pillow. Twenty-four hours each day
she was available as God's gift to a broken world, and
she said to me, "I'm so lucky to have work to do."

Everything around her had a special look. Her very
glass of water, with its flexible straw, seemed to gleam

with holy properties. The utter foolishness of her situation made the room and her garments shine white as no fuller could make them.

And when I met her my own vocal chords were paralyzed, and I knelt like an old nun with my chin on her muslin sheets and tried to breathe in some of her holiness.

Several years ago I sat in the immense papal audience room of the Vatican, where the sculptured Ascension bursts like the sun at the center of the dais; and, surrounded by the sweetest of pilgrims and nuns and monks, I watched as Pope Paul VI was carried into the room on his chair. The love that poured forth for him nearly knocked me witless, and he seemed to fix his black eyes on each of us there, calling us to Christ.

Then taking my cue from the devout Catholics around me, I, a Protestant, held up medals and crucifixes that friends had sent across the ocean with me, as the Shaman Pope raised his hands in blessing; I nodded, happily foolish, as the Prophet Pope exhorted us to better lives; I smiled an ecumenical smile as the Lover Pope beamed in his ancient office with the joy of Jesus.

He was like an old Spode teacup: fragile, precious, gleaming with the polish of God's Spirit, thinned by surrender. He died a month later; Vive Il Papa! What a delirium of holiness a pope must have to maintain: a puff of white smoke, and he rules the hearts and rites of millions. Would he have said, like the man who anointed me, "My blessing is only a sacramental act"?

"What news, Father? Good news?"

"Yea, daughter, for I believe!"

He would not say, "only sacramental," because although the anointing minister was a *good* man, the pope was a holy one; and holy men and women know that "only sacramental" means only everything. I knew holiness the minute I saw his white porcelain cheeks.

How do you and I get holy, anyhow? Where is Holy? Is there a pool I can jump into and come out sacred or sinless?

"Yes," affirms a perfect E-major chord, sung by a small cloud of angels drifting by my head. "You jumped into it when you were baptized."

But I'm not holy or sinless now. Oh, if I had reached out and touched the fringe of Pope Paul's cape, would I have been healed of arthritis or a caustic tongue, or made impervious to temptation? How do I get my hands on Aaron's sons, to be made like them? How do I go and sin no more?

"I know Holy when I see it. But I don't know how to be it," I tell Christ. "Could I settle for radical obedience?"

"Oh, Great Qwerty!" interrupts the middle-aged editor who crawls out from under my computer keyboard. "That sounds dangerous. And awfully, well, . . . literal."

Lord, in your mercy, hear my prayer: if Christianity isn't dangerous, if there is no risk, if it isn't radical and literal about feeding the hungry and telling the truth and scraping the sawdust out of your own eye, and grounded in the fact that one hot spring night, during Passover, some people conspired to kill God—then I don't want it.

Lord, in your mercy, hear my prayer: I believe, help my unbelief; I love, help my unlove; I crave holiness, in spite of the fact that I have said I will settle for less; help my unholiness.

"Don't get it mixed up with decency or social acceptability," shouts a voice from the tiny silver crucifix near my bedside table. "Sarah was lousy, you know. Had tent-fleas jumping all over the place. Rubbed sheep tallow on her hair to make it shine."

"But she believed," I said.

"When she saw," said Jesus, jumping down to my level. "Like Thomas. I had to lay Isaac in her arms for her to really believe."

"Well, she *was* pretty old to start having babies," I tell him. "Look. I want to believe without seeing. But sometimes I stand, like Sarah, snickering in my tent, right in earshot of the Most High. Sometimes. I want to believe. I want to think that every word about you in the Bible is absolutely, inerrantly true."

"Why? Will that make you either more holy or more obedient? Don't hassle inerrancy; just trust me, okay?"

"Okay, then, make me holy," I tell him, finding that the right side of my lip has a tendency to curl into a snarl if I don't keep it pulled down.

"Make yourself holy," he answers, laughing, as usual. "I already did the groundwork on that hill outside Jerusalem. The rest is up to you, but make sure it's what you want. You start down the path to radical obedience, which is only another name for holiness, and you'll find there ain't no turning back."

"I'm scared," I confess.

"Good," he says. "That's the beginning of wisdom. I'm a consuming fire, remember? I want everything. It is a terrible thing to fall into the hands of the Living God."

"I thought it was supposed to quit being terrible once you got converted. Was I ever converted?"

"Constantly!" he cries. "I keep converting you and changing you every time your guard is down." And then he went out of my seeing and hearing, off again on some cosmic mission, very likely on my own behalf.

Well, it *is* a terrible thing to fall into his hands. You let God get started and there's no stopping him. Give God an inch, or two-point-five-four centimeters or whatever, and he'll take more than a kilometer. He'll take everything exposed, everything available in body or mind or spirit. No matter how holy or obedient I think I have become, he'll never be satisfied until I am dressed in a wedding garment.

What if Today, God's Day, came now? Is Jesus really still hanging up there, safely, serenely crucified on my bedroom wall? Or—what is that bright, thin cloud moving on the horizon of my consciousness?

Well, even so, come, Lord Jesus! because tattered and dirty as my garments still are today, I cannot resist the thought of seeing him with more than my mind's eye. He is irresistible: as dolphins dive with abandon into the holy waters that surround them, so I leap into the arms of Christ.

Forgive me, Lord. I have soiled the shining clothes you put on me at baptism. We failed in stewardship, my spouse and I, by letting a marauder kill one of your creatures, and then we reached for blame to hurl at each other. I also nursed angry thoughts about a friend. I resented having aching knees, and shook my fist at heaven. How do I stop this?

The answer lies for me where the answer always lies for all of us, of course: not in extended penances or exquisitely painful mortifications or even in groveling as a miserable sinner before the throne of God, but in worship. It lies in death.

Dying to sin, or crucifying sin, as Paul was wont to phrase it, consists of dying to any consciousness of oneself, even of one's own sin.

Unfortunately, most of the pilgrims I have met along the way are too preoccupied with their own sin. They say, "More of Jesus, less of me" but are trying too hard to do the work themselves, to make room for Jesus. They speak of the fruits of the Holy Spirit in their lives but then proceed to try to plant and prune and cultivate these fruits themselves, as if they were a reward for hard work instead of the harvest of the Spirit's work, God's own action, within us.

If one plants dichondra in a grass lawn, it will ultimately choke out the grass. One needn't kill the grass first; in fact, the herbicide we use to kill grass might also injure dichondra (or Irish moss or whatever exotic ground cover). One need not worry so about self; we will die to self if we allow ourselves to be choked out by the enormous presence of this maniac lover of a God. Plant Jesus Christ in your heart and he grows there until even the tiniest weed-patch is quietly overrun.

And now I think the worshiper in me just rose up, called by the sound of some distant music, some fragile cloud of incense; for what did the Law teach me except sin? And if I look at my sins, if I throw it into the fire and melt it, what happens, nonny nonny?

"And [Aaron] said to them, 'Let any who have gold take it off'; so they gave it to me, and I threw it into the fire, and there came out this calf."

I wasn't doing anything, Lord; this golden calf, this monument to my pride, this Mount Rushmore of egotism and unholiness, just popped right out of the fire. So if I take off the earrings of my vanity and melt them, saying that I want to see the evidence of my forgiveness, what comes out of the fire? A special kind of idolatry: negative narcissism created by fascination with my own unworthiness.

"Does that mean I can ignore my sins?" asks the ugly little chigger under the skin on the inside of my wrist. No, Scratch, it does not; and quit trying, Lucifer, thou fallen star, to put words into God's holy mouth. It means I should confess and get forgiven as quickly as possible. As you well know, you Enemy. Any kind of guilt beyond that is not only neurotic; it's spiritually arrogant.

"Okay," says a more welcome voice. "Confess, so we can get on with the Dance."

"All right," I say, trembling. The Adversary is before the throne today; the Prosecuting Attorney is hard at work. He paces back and forth, rubbing his hands in anticipation of my downfall, which would humiliate Christ.

"She spoke in great anger to her husband," hisses the Accuser. "She nursed a grudge. She told a lie on two occasions and evaded the truth on a third. She complained about your weather. She even ignored someone in trouble last week; probably it was Jesus," he ends, his eyes sparkling as he tells God about it.

"How about it?" asks God. "Did you do all that?"

"Yes," I say quickly; for I remember as he speaks that Jesus told us to "agree with your adversary quickly." If I deny the Devil's accusations or try to defend myself, then I am a fool, and not one of Christ's fools, either. As soon as I plead guilty, my own advocate steps forward.

"One of mine," he whispers to his Father, and I hear the verdict: "No condemnation."

"When you are filled with me, there will be room for nothing else," he reminds me. "Don't dwell on a forgiven sin; instead, follow me."

I lean back in the everlasting arms and feel my mouth fill and sweeten with the nectar of his name. The world turns the color of him, and my own sin seems unimportant.

"Hand it here," he whispers, and I give him not only that newly-forgiven package of fresh sin, but some others I usually ignore.

"Now, look at holiness," he says.

When I was a young girl it was popular for people to say to one another in moments of sinful despair, "Look on the bright side." Bright Side! The glimpse of glory, just beyond that hill, behind that cloud, raised above that altar. The host lifted, the chalice elevated, a million Mass bells tinkling in heaven and earth. The gleam of the cup's silver and gold is a blinding Bright Side.

"If one's eye is single, the whole body is full of Bright Sides," says Christ to his Church. "Come, my sister, my

Bride! Don't stand there before a mirror, fretting about a pimple on your chin, when the Bridegroom is at the door, waiting to embrace you."

Perhaps we put on our wedding garments for the wrong reasons. Do I try to keep the garment of righteousness mended and clean for him, or is all this industry to impress the other guests? This is a monumental risk, this access to God, this narrow way. What if I fall off the road into the abyss?

"Don't look down," he says, pulling my chin up. "You can't fall if you look up. Follow the gleam."

I see them assembled at the top of the winding road: my own house has been moved there, and the wedding guests, dressed in rainbows, wait on the front step. Angels, Archangels, Cherubim, Seraphim, and all the company of heaven stand on the entry walk. Their sleepless eyes are fixed, not on the Bride nor on her blemishes, but on him who has eyes of fire.

"I am not worthy to meet with these," I whisper. "And I am not worthy that thou shouldst come under my roof."

But he laughs. The company of heaven will never know whether I am worthy or not. They will never even see me, those whose faces are constantly turned to the countenance of God.

More of Jesus, less of me? The only way I know to make that happen is to clean up as fast as possible and join the crowd of worshipers, to look at him, to adore him, to respond to him, to be totally filled. I must be made holy by touching the original holiness.

As I finished typing that last line, I stopped to take a sip of coffee; and I know Jesus is laughing. Round and round my cup is printed "KRIS KRIS KRIS KRIS." O, Lord, we are so funny! I ask him, "If I can be made holy only by fixing my mind on you, then why don't I have a cup that says, 'JESUS JESUS JESUS JESUS JESUS'?"

"You do," he says, growing solemn, and holds out his cup, daring me to drink.

Ah. His draught stings the lips, sears the throat, and is deadly to worldly desire. The spirit within me longs to drink eternal Life. Poison to self. More of Jesus.

Worship him now, in the beauty of his holiness, because next time he appears, it will be (as C. S. Lewis says) "without disguise."

Then God the Unleashed Lover will give even more of himself away in a new and fiery mercy. Love is his power, wild as electricity and as untamed as high heaven. You don't believe it? Look at lightning, shredding up the ionosphere, and then think what unleashed, unconditional Love will do to our small, plastic lives.

The psalmist cries, Let the whole earth stand in awe of him; and the raped planet, the furrowed, final earth, groaning in travail for her own salvation, cries back, Amen! Amen! Amen!

But without the presence of God the Redeemer, who could abide the God of Creation? Who would be able to stand that untamed love, this time untempered by doubt or physical Incarnation or systematic theology? But thanks to God for God's mercy, for with his madness comes also his blessing, if only we will embrace the feet of Christ.

A Greek wrote about it, long before the birth of Jesus. In the *Bacchae*, one of the darkest of Euripides' tragedies, the god Dionysos came to Thebes disguised as a beautiful young man. He had come kindly to temper their passions with love, saying, "Bring me all that wildness in your hearts: I understand it. As my brother, Apollo, told you, Know yourselves. You have great need of me."

But the people of Thebes, especially the women, rejected him, saying that they lived in a city with laws and had no need of him. "You would make wild beasts of us!" they said; and finally Pentheus, the protagonist, cut off the beautiful "boy's" hair and then demanded his thyrsos.

Now, thyrsos is the madness of a god or goddess: it is raw power; and in ancient Greek tradition, each person must choose some god's thyrsos, thus fulfilling one's own nature by devotion to that madness. If an individual's devotion is true, a god or goddess will accompany madness with blessing to gentle and channel it.

But when the Thebans rejected him, Dionysos, in a wrath, left them his madness, all right, but without any blessing.

"And that is why," ends Euripides, "the Thebans became mad, unholy, running on the mountains and tearing at live wolves with their bare hands."

I sat on a grassy hillside as a young girl and listened to a college production of this play, and my heart burned within me. Madness without blessing! Is that what happened to Lucifer, the runaway child of morning?

But although Dionysos left the mountainsides of Thebes without his love remaining, Christ offers both: thyrsos, agape. Behold, I stand at the door and knock.

"Perhaps the Holy Spirit is the thyrsos of God," suggests the teasing red lizard that wraps itself around the leg of my desk, its tongue darting.

Away, reptile; do not tempt me. I have no time for theory, being occupied with the fact of God.

"I thought you said that sometimes you didn't really believe," it says, its colorless eyes big with malice.

"Get thee behind me," I shout, rapping it with a sheaf of paper, wondering why people don't any longer keep inkwells to throw at the Devil. It's not just a matter of belief: God will be God whether or not I ask him to be. But how do I gain his blessing too?

"When you are full of me, there will be no more room for anything else," he says, one more time; and I suddenly know blessing.

John's First Epistle reminds us that God is greater than our consciences, which may have been built by human hands; and I can testify that his blessing is far greater than my sense of sin. Once removed from sin by his blessing, I am, we are, made whole and real.

Look at the work of the Late Father Louis, Thomas Merton. When he wrote *The Seven Storey Mountain*, he had already been a Trappist monk for some years. The first half of that book is stiff and unconvincing, because it shows the "before" picture, the life of Merton the sinner. Because Merton was living in blessing when he wrote, neither he nor God could remember exactly how those sins felt. But lo! when he began to tell of his love for God in the monastery, the descriptions of Communion, the early mornings in company with the Cistercian fathers—one begins to soar with the reading, for at this point he writes about what is real, about what has for him become the only reality.

God, putting our sins away from us, makes them strangers even in the graves we dig in our backyards. Thanking him for a state of grace, I finger the rosary that I secret in the pocket of my Protestant blue jeans, and I hear him behind me. Or rather, I hear the whirlwind inside me speak, and I turn in rapture.

"Dance," he whispers joyfully, and I do.

One of the things Andrew's grandmother does, beside write things down and cavort under the filberts and play with a goat, is to listen to a great deal of music. Sometimes this music is classical, but sometimes it's rock and roll, to the absolute despair of some of my Christian friends.

"It's from the Devil," they say, and I laugh my best Sarah laugh. Once the Church also tried to ban the playing of the violin everywhere in Europe, because the church fathers believed that it seduced, aroused primitive, Adamic passions, and pandered to the lowest in humanity. Now it's a certain brand of beats-to-the-measure that takes a whipping.

But there is nowhere God is not. If I go to the bottom of the sea or the deepest cave, if I say to a mountain, "Fall on me," if I dance down the path of Bach or Wagner or a rock band with him, he is there.

I place a ten-year-old tape by the Hollies on my player, and hear them say, "Sometiiiiimmesss . . . all I need is the air that I breathe, yes, to love you. . . ."

Yeah. Oh, yeah. Sometimes all I need is the air, whether it's the sweet spring air of spring or the carbon-laden gust of city wind, to love him. Just enough air, enough breath, to say the Name. . . .

And just as in his house there are many mansions, so in his Dance are forms infinitely various, infinitely beautiful; as differentiated is his Dance as are galaxies, snowflakes, petals, eyes, fingers, nebulae, spores, follicles, calyxes, prayers. We come in our own predestined and elected time and grace, leaping or bowing, gliding or tapping, wearing perfect, shining costumes of reticence or boldness, speaking or singing, sighing or shouting: we each wear a garment that will fit no one except oneself, for it is made by putting on Christ.

Ah! Jesus seizes my hands and dances me through the universe in the same infinitely split second in which he lifts ancient Sarah out of her rock tomb in Machpelah; and he whispers tenderly, "Sarah, laugh again for me, my darling."

"Laugh? Laugh for doubt again?" asks Simple Simon, at the edge of mystery in my head. No, Simple. Laughs like an angel for forgiveness and belief does Sarah, as her four-thousand-year-old feet climb out of the rocks in Hebron, and lets her hair, growing ever so much more lovely by the second, float on the scented wind from the south; and straining, only a little now, to hear, she catches the sound of the Lord's trumpet, and perhaps a Lion's roar: and she leaps gloriously into the splendor of his music.

All is forgiven everyone, Sarah. It's Easter Sunday forever, Sarah; the dishes are eternally washed, the dinner is always cooked, and there is nothing for a woman in love or a daughter of Adam to do except to dance and be holy. And laugh.

VII
MALE AND FEMALE
CREATED HE THEM

For I am sure that neither death, nor life, nor angels, nor principalities, nor things present, nor things to come, nor powers, nor height, nor depth, nor anything else in all creation, will be able to separate us from the love of God in Christ Jesus our Lord. (Romans 8:38)

Alas, my Lord! A Martha sweeps her daughter's empty room; a Mary sits now to listen, but not to the voice of his love. Instead, she has chosen a lesser love, more accessible, with less chance of being burnt in God's fire.

A girl fifteen, the daughter of a friend, has quit school and left home to live with a Lesbian many years older than herself. Her family, though relieved of some of the strain of a year-long quarrel, is nonetheless devastated. Sappho, you daughter of Lilith, how could you?

Will the girl's father and mother still love this child, now that she lives a life they consider strange and abominable? Will she seem ugly and tainted to them now? If she comes to dinner, will they boil her plate and silverware to stop the growth of germs that might invade and infect their other children?

And what now of the other daughter? She is thirteen, with penetrating hazel eyes and a funny, sobbing little laugh: what of her? What of her brother, older, golden-eyed, beautiful, carrying the burden of his sister's defection silently, as he might carry a book into a room and lay it down noiselessly: what of him? Is there anything we can say to them lest they too run with flaming minds and thighs into the hot streets?

Another friend, a maiden woman in her seventies, a retired professor, recently wept for this girl, and for all who struggle with singleness and wholeness in a society that has taught us the importance of pairing. She and I sat and ate gingerbread and drank cups and cups of coffee, to overcome the steamy and suffocating effects of a long church-school teachers' meeting. As she talked, tears crept from the inner corners of her eyes and she shook her head: I saw seventy years of misjudged innocence grabbing at her lower jaw.

"One dares not to be single," she said, "or one is suspect." In her case, since she has always been beautiful and brilliant and charming, nobody has ever suggested that she might be single by choice; people have wondered if she were also Gay, or had a secret lover, or was perhaps for some reason kept from her true calling as a nun.

"Two women I have known for years, colleagues, also retired, were lonely in their middle age," she murmured, her hand stilled in the air over her gingerbread, like a blessing. "So they bought a house together. Now the department head constantly refers to them as 'those two old dykes.' They aren't Gay, but if they were, would he have to speak that way?"

"It's cruel, cruel," I agreed in my best coffeebreak voice. What arrogance: how would I know? I am not single, and when I was divorced, in my early forties, I made it obvious to everyone who knew me that I was miserable in my heterosexual singleness.

"When are we, as Christians, going to be honest about the sexual struggle?" she said. "We hate singleness. For years, I was treated like an appendage to my parents. Both of them were old and sick, and at church people would say, 'Hello-how's-your-mother-today?' I had no place in the church—a woman who had never married. I wasn't very interested in the bazaar, and nobody suggested I might do something else."

She *did* do something else; she did a great deal of else. She lives far up in the woods, and for many years a house church met in her wonderful log home. Now she finds ways to let young people in school, or couples trying to start over, or former convicts, come and share her life and work. And she drives over the mountains in fall, winter, and summer, in a 1966 Karman Ghia, to teach college classes to inmates at the state prison.

Some singles drop out. They go to church until they are twenty, and then finally give up; here in this Oregon town, some of them turn up a few years later at a huge local neopentecostal church where singleness is considered normal and good.

And I have known presidents of guilds, and altar guild members, and church school teachers, women into everything, who never missed a service of any kind; and then they got widowed or divorced, and after a few tries at what they considered "normal life" (but now they worked and the two oldest children were grown) never returned to his table. If they remarry, they sometimes turn back up in a pew, holding the new man by the arm, now respectably coupled again.

One of my own daughters chose not to marry until she was twenty-nine. She lived in a beautiful apartment, and worked, and dated, and saw women friends, and read, and came to family gatherings; and for more than ten years she tried to find her place in the Church. She grew to hate the coffee hour because of the gushy assumption that there was a reason she didn't have a man. One April weekend we went to a parish growth retreat together, and she poured out her annoyance.

"Because I don't have a husband, you treat me like a second-class citizen," she told the parishioners gathered there. "You expect me to be the person who takes care of the church nursery during the service every week, so you can keep me out of sight. I seem to be a blot on your record of matchmaking."

Shocked, they stared at her and carefully missed the point. "We'll have to be more loving," said one woman.

"I don't need more love," she answered, gentling. "I know you love me. But you love me as if I am still adolescent because I don't have a husband. Use me in the work of the Church as a grown woman."

What she did not say, out of regard for the sincerity and innocence of the other people there, was that she would also prefer that people not seem to supervise her private life.

"If I were married, nobody would wonder what I do with my sexuality," she told me. "But the whole parish acts as if it has a right to administer my privacy, like letting a child have certain privileges and withholding others until I'm a real grownup."

One of our friends recently removed himself from the mainstream of singleness by returning to the Gay life; he had spent years in celibacy and mental vacillation and prayer and sorrow. One day he said, "I can't do it."

Because he was a minister, he left his parish church; but his denomination let him retain his papers, and he is sometimes guest minister at various parishes and sometimes does a wedding or a funeral. He has gone to live with another dear friend of mine, also come to the end of his celibacy.

The second friend came here yesterday to drink herbal tea and quarrel lovingly.

"You'll just have to accept me as I am," he said. "God made me this way, and I'm tired of living like a monk."

"Well, you'll just have to accept me too," I answered. Our voices were high and clear as foxes' barks in a winter dawn. "You want to do as you must; now let me suffer if I must."

"Suffering is not a necessity of life."

"Neither is sex," I insisted. "Nobody died of celibacy."

"But they can die of loneliness and despair," he said, and my heart tripped slightly, remembering loneliness, remembering despair.

And to make it all harder, there is no real practiced Christian standard of behavior, at least not in this side of the Church, irrespective of what our pre-Sexual Revolution assumptions may have been. Perhaps in the more conservative evangelical Church the rules are a little clearer; but those of us in the mainstream do not seem to know for certain what we believe about nonmarital sex or homosexuality; there is no sexual paragraph that we can stand up and say on Sunday morning in the way that we make our theological statements in the recitation of the Nicene Creed.

"Do you really want a systematic theology of sex?" taunts Thomas Aquinas from the pocket of my Lay Reader's alb. "You're always quarreling with systematic theologians. Now you want to use them for your own ends."

Is that what we want? Do we want to rise up and say, facing the altar, "We believe in carnal conjunction between man and woman (or boy and girl or man and man)"? It would take more than Constantine locking the bishops in to get us to come up with a statement we could all embrace: there might be a giant exodus of any given group, organized or otherwise, whose lifestyle was eliminated as "belief," or whose more proscriptive sensibilities were offended.

No, thorough Tom, I cannot use theology this time to achieve my ends, because I do not know my own ends. I seem to believe something and yet react in diametric opposition. It's easy to be glib about Gays or unmarried couples who live together or married people who commit adultery unless you happen to love some of them. Then everything becomes complicated.

I came into my bedroom after the tea party and sat for a long time on the edge of my bed, thinking about the sins of the flesh.

"Help me!" I shouted at my crucifix.

His voice sounded like notes dropped from a silver flute. "What?"

"Don't just hang up there being ornamental," I yelled. "Come down to earth and help me understand."

I think he raised an eyebrow; at any rate, I apologized for being demanding and rude.

"It's all right. I'm glad you called," he said, jumping down beside me; and so I asked him again about my two Gay friends.

"According to some parts of the Bible, they're going to hell," I said.

"According to some parts, so are you," he retorted with love. "But if anyone sins, they have an advocate with the Father."

"Well, but they say it's not a sin. That's my whole quandary."

"It isn't your job to worry about whether others are sinful," he said gently. "The ability I created in you is to love unconditionally. But if you feel so strongly, why didn't you say so honestly when they were here for dinner last week, or when he was here today?"

"I was afraid of *being* judgmental," I said.

"Wro-o-n-ng," rang Christ the Fonz. "Wrong. You weren't afraid of being judgmental. You were afraid of *sounding* judgmental. And you were afraid they'd get mad and reject you."

"You mean I should have said what I thought?"

"The truth shall set you free," he suggested.

"Free of friends," I told him.

"I know," he murmured.

"You mean, I should have said, 'You're both nuts; God didn't make you this way, you're kidding yourself'? I can't do that. I don't want to offend them; and besides, I can't be sure I have the truth by the tail."

"Then don't try to bring about the work of their salvation. Their redemption is my job, not yours. Look. I'll show you what I'm going to do for you. For you and the Gays and the kids shacking up and the couples who have been married fifty years."

"Show me," I said, holding my breath. He climbed back up on the silver cross over my nightstand and stretched his body out in eternal intercession.

VIII
SUBDUING THE EARTH

Dance, O earth, at the presence of the Lord, at the presence of the God of Jacob, who turned the rock into a pool of water, the granite cliff into a fountain. (Psalm 114:7-8, NEB)

When I started to write this book, Andrew was two years old; as I write this chapter he is just five, and he can shoot a ball into a basket and say long words like "awesome" and "nevertheless." And in these nearly three years, our yard has gone completely feral.

After all, this is only about a third of an acre, I thought on the morning of August eighth. Surely we could do better than this, especially for my son's wedding rehearsal dinner, to be held on our back deck that night.

The weeds were rampant, trees needed trimming, the deck was a mess, and all this became part of a spirited discussion between my husband and me, which means there was some arm-waving and some yelling.

Because I am allergic to bee sting, I rarely go outdoors in full day of summer. My communion with the Lord God through his creation is most often in the very early morning or evening, during bee-sleep hours, or in the rain, when bees do something else I don't know about.

At any rate, I went out at about six in the morning in a mood of search and destroy, and began to survey the estate. My husband followed me, looking hagridden

and hunted: my opinions about our homestead sometimes give rise to orgies of physical work, which he
hates.

"You're compulsive," he told me. "A workaholic.
And now you want me to be one too."

"Look at this," I said, waving my arm at the back
corner where brambles held full sway. "These black-
berry vines have to go."

"Okay," he said, resigned, and went to get the lopping shears. I noted that these thorny invaders were
loaded with berries. I ate sixteen immediately and put
twenty more into my big coffee mug.

"Squaw!" screamed a giant crow: I think I was in his
territory.

"Watch out who you're calling a squaw, there, chau-
vinist," I said, waving a broom at him. He didn't even
flinch. My husband reappeared, ready to cut.

"I guess they can stay," I said. "After all, there *is*
edible fruit on them. Just cut off the big suckers that
might catch people's feet. And get rid of that crow
before he eats our profits."

My husband eyed the crow; the crow cocked its head,
nodded almost imperceptibly, and flew away.

"I just visualize myself holding a gun and looking
through the sights. They always leave," he said, swear-
ing to it. He also seems to understand chickens and
hermit crabs, in a different way.

"Weeds, weeds," I said, advancing on what had been
a flower bed before the ducks ate everything. Now the
space was overtaken by weeds; and as I walked up, an
early ray of light came through the fence and struck the
head of one of the many blooms of creamy Queen
Anne's lace. The magenta milk vetch lay indolent
against the warm fenceboards. Great golden poppies
were just opening their cups.

"Well," I said, looking at the exquisite row of blos-
soms; and I sang the hundredth Psalm, the *Jubilate Deo*:

"Be joyful in the LORD, all ye lands; serve the LORD with gladness, and come before his presence with a song. . . ."

"Maybe you could just yank out the thistle rosettes," I said, and my husband raised his eyebrows and then smiled as he went to get gloves and a weed-puller. I took the loppers.

"These trees are horrible. We should cut off the ends of all limbs that are loaded with nuts, before they fall," I said as an aside to the goat as I let her out of her pen. She headed straight for a filbert tree and stood on her hind legs to nibble leaves, branch, and nuts, all in one mouthful.

I put down the loppers and looked up: there were at least four squirrels, leaping from branch to branch like the Flying Wallendas. Each had a nut in its paws, as did the bluejays in their beaks, hopping and with shrill voices daring someone to stop them. Amahl, our sixteen-pound cat, came lounging forward on his extra-toed paws. He eyed the squirrels; they looked at him and chattered. He made as if to climb a tree, sighed, and lay down, too fat to climb or care. I put down my loppers and sang "We Plow the Fields And Scatter," and the goat did one of her mid-air gymnastic turns.

"Do you want these trees trimmed?" asked my husband, hopelessness welling up in his voice.

"No, just rake up the newest nuts so the lawn mower will go," I said. I could hear my oven timer ringing indoors. "Let's eat breakfast first."

We penned the goat and went inside. I took the bread out of the oven and sang "Break Thou the Bread of Life." Then we said grace and read the sixth chapter of the Gospel According to John. We drank coffee and ate the twenty blackberries and some eggs our hens had laid, talked about the Gospel lesson, and looked at each other shyly about "Bread" as we ate from a loaf just out of the oven.

My daughter Carol arrived, looking, as usual, like an English portrait. She was wearing her jeans.

"I came to clean the deck and set up the tables," she said. "I woke up and started thinking about you making that buffet for thirty people, so I came to clean up."

"You needn't," I said weakly, but she smiled brilliantly, grabbed a cup of coffee, and went for the broom and hose. I followed her out and we sang "Day by Day." My husband looked less miserable as he went to finish the nuts. By then the sun was out in full and I feared bees, so I made my trip around the front yard a quick one.

The grass, of course, needed mowing; and the roses were out of hand because they had not got pruned the winter before. I always imagine that someday I will have a topiarial yard, something like the palace at Versailles, with boxwood mazes and rose trees and raised herb beds full of southernwood and lavender and mother-of-thyme and symmetrically cascading rosemary, where everything is controlled and perfect. Instead, our roses leaned out and over and touched the ground like an untidy waterfall, and there were several unidentified mushrooms here and there in the lawn and under the unruly corkscrew willow.

I got my mushroom book and determined that the mushrooms were Rosy Gomphidius and one questionable Stropharia. Good grief! That last sounds like a grammatical error, I thought; and then I began to write a book: "The rosy gomphidious dawn came rising. . . ."

A fur-coated bumblebee zoomed nearby, and I came to consciousness and retreated indoors; the telephone was ringing anyhow. It was Kimberley, my son's bride-to-be, a dark, lovely, lithe girl with hair to her hips; my son has courted her for about four years.

She wanted to make sure I didn't cut off the faded roses, since she wanted to scatter rose petals all over the aisle of the church. She and my son also wanted to thank me for everything, *everything*, including my late father's ring: his name was Frank, and my son's name is Frank, and it seemed fitting that he should have his grandfather's signet ring. Kim melted it down in her jewelry class and made a wedding band for her groom.

"And then, any more roses you have, we'll put in the church." They scorned a florist, and gathered wild flowers from the fields, piecing them out with ivy and donations from yards. She thanked me one more time for everything; and then my husband came in.

"If you want, you can shake the rose bushes for petals," I told him. He looked goatishly interested; some of the sorrow was leaving the curve of his cheek. We went out and, watching very carefully for bees, shook enough petals to cover the aisle at Canterbury. I thought about our crazed, wild-growing roses and their place at the wedding, so I sang "Immortal, Invisible, God Only Wise."

Ron went to look for the Japanese lanterns to string in the trees. "Decide what we should do in front too," he said, fearfully. I dared not touch the roses now: God had spoken. But at the front of the yard a fir tree had volunteered, and now it was almost three feet tall.

The tree had to go. Stewardship and ecology notwithstanding, I decided, that little scraggly tree was of no beauty. And to top it off, an orb-weave spider had made a great web all over it. I went for the lopping shears.

"Grandmother?"

The small voice belonged to Justin, now also five years old, like Andrew. Because he is Andrew's friend, and plays with him, and hears Andrew call me, he has assumed that my given name is Grandmother. (Which, in the finest sense of "given," it is.)

"Grandmother?"

"Yes, Justin?" I said, as I advanced on the stringy fir tree.

"Did you know a spider decorated your Christmas tree?"

I put down the loppers. Carol came out, and we three took hands and sang "Jingle Bells" in the August sun.

"What about the yard?" asked Ron, apprehension making the corners of his mouth twitch.

"Just mow the lawn, and then we'll put up the lanterns," I said. Susan came, her wonderful long hair making damp curls at her neck; she and Carol and I did the cooking and arranged tables on the deck, hauling out candles and cloths and silverware. Andrew and Justin and some other little boys rode bikes and shrieked with joyous abandon in the cul-de-sac while the sun caught my kitchen prism and sent thousands of rainbows swimming like giant neon tetras on the walls.

The girls left to dress, and my husband came in for a late lunch, sweat in a fine sheen on his body. Grass clippings clung to his skin like a thin fur.

"Come talk to me while I hang the lanterns," he said, and I sang a chorus of the ancient *Phos Hilaron*: "O gracious Light, pure brightness of the everliving Father in heaven. . . ."

"I'll read to you," I called up to him. He stood on a ladder with his upper body hidden in the filbert tree; as he stepped down to move the ladder I read aloud, "The grass withereth, the flower fadeth, but the word of our God shall stand forever. . ." (KJV).

IX
THROUGH THE CURTAIN

So now, my friends, the blood of Jesus makes us free to enter boldly into the sanctuary by the new, living way which he has opened for us through the curtain, the way of his flesh. (Hebrews 10:19-20, NEB)

There was a time when only one man (certainly no woman) might venture into the Holy of Holies. In fact, even the high priest of Israel had a rope around his waist when he went beyond the veil so that, if he were struck dead because God would not accept his sin-tainted sacrifice, the other priests could drag him out without profaning the place themselves.

But now all that is changed. We have another, a permanent High Priest who, having once and for all offered himself for us, continuously offers himself to us.

"Come in here where it's holy!" he shouts as we pass, like a carnival huckster peddling grace as if it were cheap, as if it had not cost him his life.

What I didn't know, when I first accepted his carney-barker's invitation, is that once we go in there where it's holy, we tend to get holy. And then we carry holiness with us in the person of Christ wherever we go. And to the world, his broken body is shocking and the risen Christ is overwhelming.

"Give them milk, not meat! Make him easier to read about," suggests the sensible publisher, shaped like a business card, from a pocket of my shirt.

"I can't *make* him any way," I cry. "He is what he is. He said 'I AM what I will be,' and all that. And he's within me, wherever I go."

"Really? Then God is in his creation and is his creation," says the tiny Irish mystic who sometimes jumps out of my Bible, and with whom I constantly quarrel, lovingly, about transcendence and immanence.

No, dear Celt. I am not the book I write, and God is not his own creature. Perhaps people may say of my writing, "There's a lot of you in there," but the me that someone might find in my work is a static me, unconversant, unable to relate or respond. And in my work there is really nothing subtracted from the whole of me.

However, I'll admit that God does seem to have invested an awfully lot of himself in what he made.

"Toldya," says the Irish one. "You'll get it sooner or later. All creation is holy because it was made by and in Christ, so it was and is holy."

This is a wonderful discussion; but it is another whole book. I send the mystic in me back to read all of Deuteronomy again, and I contemplate the mystery of incarnational life. Finally in desperation, I call out to Christ for an answer.

"I thought we had this conversation," he said.

"I think it's the only conversation we ever have," I admitted. "I want to know everything. I want to come out of Father Abraham's bosom like Lazarus and tell the world the answer to every dilemma."

"When I last saw him, Father Abraham said to tell you that the world has already had Moses and the prophets," he said. "And T. S. Eliot has already capitalized on the line. But what you need to know is this: that you are a part of me."

"Then—then I must suffer with you?" I ask, my breath short; and he nods, almost hesitant, hating my pain, loving my redemption.

"Ah! It is then no accident, no quirk of poor scholarship, that the translators of the Bible sometimes turned the Greek 'martyrias' into 'witness'?"

"No accident."

"And Peter is saying in his First Letter that to suffer is to have your mind? To know pain in your name must be to witness—or at least glimpse—you within ourselves?"

"Read about it," he tells me, and I read that a virgin shall conceive and bear a son.

And I see the pain of their assent, hers and his, even to the idea of it all, both Virgin and Son. For her, it was the offering up of any choice in the matter, and handing it over to as unlikely an authority as the vision of an angel.

"Yes!" Mary breathed, still not sure of the details. "Let it be done to me as you have said."

This Yes, this yielding of one's rationality, of one's right to say No, is not found everywhere. She might have said, "It's my body, and I can decide what will happen to it," and the wise world would have nodded, affirming her assertiveness. Instead, she assented to God's Will. He found perfect obedience in a little Galilean maiden. And what did Mary get as her reward for saying Yes? She got a life of total pain.

First, she had to tell her espoused husband that she was pregnant. That must have been some scene. She couldn't even articulate the entire event to his undoubtedly-shocked countenance, but she kept things in her heart and pondered them, and had to trust God for the rest.

Then she gave birth, not in a decent bed, but in a stable, unattended by any but her husband and some animals.

("But the host of heaven was there," cries the Romantic who swims through the right ventricle of my heart.

("The host of heaven is here too, and I'm still looking for earthly approval," I retort, breathing slower to make her shut up and swim.)

And the culmination of Mary's painful life, the final installment of her total obedience, the apex of her affirmative response to God, was to stand at the foot of the cross and watch her Son die an exquisitely painful death.

And what about the Son's holy pain? For the Son, pain did not begin with the cross: it had to begin, it must have begun, the day he stepped off the throne and became incarnate, not only as a man, but first as an embryo in a woman's body, and then as a helpless baby. C. S. Lewis suggests that if we want to get the hang of what it was like for Christ, we must imagine becoming something like a slug or a crab.

I for one am sorry that my own denomination rarely bends its knee any more at the words "And he became incarnate" in the Nicene Creed. My own introspection on the importance of God's daring in becoming a man came to me originally when I began to ponder this liturgical genuflection. The Church said, *"et incarnatus est"* and for centuries dropped to its knees. One day I finally wondered why I was kneeling and upon investigation ended up knowing him. But nowadays we rarely genuflect. Instead, we sometimes bow, or look at our Prayer Books or even at each other.

But Christ reminds me that, as we have fewer and fewer opportunities to act out the Confession of Awe, we redeem the time with an increased inner holiness; and this brings me back to suffering, and to his suffering.

There is a kind of suffering in the life and death of Jesus that we don't talk about. But I am convinced, as I read the account of Gethsemane, that his agony had to be far more, something much more horrifying, than violent, shameful physical death.

Death comes to all who live, and God permits it, even if it was not his idea to introduce it into the world; and Jesus knew all that. Death to a man of Jesus' age was certainly not unheard-of in that century; and for that matter, neither was violent death. Roman soldiers rode their horses over children. Poverty brought theft, and theft brought murder. And even a tavern brawl often ended in death, just as it does now.

Furthermore, people did *not* leave all executions to the state, as we try to do, even though Roman law officially said they must. Sometimes they picked up stones and killed the offenders themselves. Or if they couldn't, they rushed them to the procurator, who on at least one historical occasion hung them by hundreds on crosses, where their bodies, viewed by anyone who passed, would quickly decompose in the hot climate.

So why was he more overcome by agony and despair than anyone else among us who knows that his or her time is at a stop? If death were the only future terror, then he faced no worse than what we all face: to endure pain and death, and to awaken in the presence of God. If anyone had faith in a life hereafter, this one should have.

So why did he throw himself down under the olive trees and beg, while sweat rolled off his forehead like clots of blood? What was it he feared most?

Even in John's long account of Jesus in his last hours with the disciples, there is a sudden breach of divinity. At one moment, Jesus prays his high-priestly prayer; but suddenly he stands up, walks out, and crosses the Kidron, to become vulnerable to sin, to death, to agony, to despairing of his Father's love. The great gulf between heaven and hell is symbolized for me in his crossing of that brook. And once across, there was no turning back.

Why such terrible agony? I have never heard a preacher say this, and I have never read it in a book; but I think Jesus, now apparently cut off from full communication with his Father, believed that when the sin of the world entered him, he would go to hell for it. And stay there for it.

"The Son of Man is betrayed to sinful men," he says, as Judas approaches, in Matthew's version of the passion; he just as easily and truthfully could have said, "The Savior of humanity is now overcome by the sin of humanity."

When he became the Curse for our sake, did he believe he would endure that horror forever, so that we could live?

"Scorpion, Scorpion," I whisper, wondering. I let my own voice wonder, now: this is too gigantic to let fall out of the mouths of Dormice or Raggedy Anns or Barbies or Irish mystics or other imaginary fragments of my own mad mind.

No wonder the earth shook as he died; no wonder there was an eclipse of the sun: the whole universe was in shock as Jesus Christ, the second person of the Godhead, entered the realm of the dead! No wonder the veil in the Temple was torn in two, flapping like a bad housekeeper's tattered windowshade! God himself had become the Curse, and gone to hell.

Is this heresy? Is it possibly even blasphemy? But he did go to hell. He invaded the Magic Kingdom, the plastic Disneyland of the Spirit, where "the disobedient were waiting," as Peter says; and he harrowed it.

When we were in Istanbul, Turkey, we visited a late Byzantine basilica called The Church of Our Savior at Kariye (or Chora). And I stood for a long time, perhaps half an hour, transfixed, in front of the famous fresco of the *Anastasis*, the Resurrection. There the risen Christ stands; in his right hand is Adam and in his left, Eve;

and he is pulling them from their graves into life. He had to go to hell to get them.

"Our bus is ready to leave," said the tour guide, and my husband took a picture of the fresco so I could keep the sight forever. But I didn't need to look for that photograph when we developed all the slides, because it is, first of all, in every art textbook written; and secondly, it is so emblazoned in my mind that I could never forget it.

If he hadn't gone to hell, what exactly would have been overcome? How else would death and sin and the Curse and the Scorpion have been vanquished? The original earthly atonement in the Holy of Holies was brought about by the sprinkling of the blood of an animal that died and was consumed. So, then did the Lamb of God die—and have to be consumed, but this time by Death himself. Jesus gave himself over into the hands of Satan—and arose. Went to hell and came out of hell, dancing. The agony in the garden was overcome.

"They cut me down, and I leapt up high, for I am the Life that will never, never die," says the last verse of "The Lord of the Dance." I find, as I think of all this, that instead of dancing, my knees are weak, and my fingers shaking.

Perhaps Osiris and Tammuz, Eurydice and Persephone could be called from Sheol or Hades or the Place of the Dead only by a faithful lover and the embalmer's art, their earthly lives tied as symbols to the planting and the gathering-in. Winter to spring, the Nile flooding, and the sun crossing the vernal equinox all contributed to Isis and her journey to the underworld, or to the rise of Tammuz in the east. But did they dare try to leap up clear from the depths of hell on their own merits only?

It is too irrational to be false. I cannot but believe it: only God could make up Z yarn like this, this kind of

Jesus-from-the-dead story, this lack of cashing-in on the seasons or the harvest or even the relationship of earth to the sun and moon.

Furthermore, if it happened two thousand years ago, it happened in God's mind after that and before that. God never lived in time: time is the Devil's plumb line, used to measure his own temporary victories. The harrowing of hell will never cease, and it began before it was. Else how can I pray for those dead that I love? Else how did David say, in the one-hundred-thirty-ninth Psalm, "If I make my bed in Sheol, again I find thee there" (NEB)?

Here is the Incarnation, then: pain and victory. There is no kind of pain he does not know, having become the Curse that the writer of Deuteronomy so succinctly outlines. He has been everything bad, everything twisted and perverted and unthinkable. Worse than that, he even became, in the Curse, the kind of frail, miserable sinner I am.

Yet I find myself sometimes thinking, "Ah, but he cannot understand this!" I even get angry and accuse him of being cold to the suffering of the world.

J'accuse. I have easily, quickly, jumped to anger and blasphemy, shaking my fist at him when things went awry, like the first time I lost a suicide over the hot line, standing there with my ear numb from the telephone, listening at first to choking, and then that awful black silence that went on and on.

And I vowed never to believe in him again when I saw a loved family member enter a quasi-death of terrible illness. On the days I did admit that Christ existed, I wondered, for seven weeks, why he did not go in there, quickly, and take her from the clutches of hell (and when she was well, I upbraided God for what was past).

Recently, I found the baby duckling dead in the yard, and, fool that I am, I said in my heart, There is no God.

Once, after a fast, merciless fire in the makeshift cardboard-box village of a Mexican border town, I spent a horrible afternoon with a Lutheran pastor, looking for the bones of missing babies, and I found a tiny ulna, a forearm bone, and shook it at the sky with all the hatred one can have toward God.

"I'm sorry," I told him later. "I shouldn't have shaken that little arm bone at you. You already knew."

"I counted your shaking as the wave offering of the Levites," Christ said gently, with tears on his face. "In that moment I counted you as holy."

"O Lord, make me really holy, make me act holy. Show me real holiness," I told him, seized by compunction and love and restive devotion. "Let me walk, through you as the veil, into the forbidden Holiest Place."

"Very well," he said, "but it won't be easy. And it may not be the way you think."

And he let me sing in choirs and feast on the words that were sung. He let me minister the chalice at Communion and see life, forever given, in the reflections of the wine, and it was glorious.

But he also let me live, and see, and hear, and taste, and know, and the sights did not look holy, and the sounds were often agonizing. The baby's ulna was neither the least nor the worst of what he led me to. I held a young girl in my arms, screaming at her to live, but she died of a heroin overdose. He introduced me to an eighty-year-old woman who had been raped. He also let me kneel by the bedside of a friend whose body was riddled with cancer, like a marksman's target, and pray, "O God, make her well, or take her to you." And he let me suffer helplessly with the suffering.

During a great famine in another country, the result first of war and then of a terrible flood of the river that wiped out crops and drowned people and left the water so polluted that cholera and typhus competed with hunger for a championship of killing, I tried one night to watch the news while eating dinner. The camera focused on an old, old man, howling with agony as he looked at his flooded rice fields and at the swollen bodies of his dead wife and daughter and grandchildren, photographed in full color. And he howled also for the pain of hunger in his own empty belly.

I began to cry, and, ashamed of my food, I pushed my plate back to lay my head on the table.

"Just wait," I sobbed to my husband. "In a little while some dilettante friend of mine will call for a donation to feed them."

Sure enough, in an hour a friend called and asked me both to donate to a relief fund and to work on the telephone fund-raising operation.

"I'll mail you a check," I said, asking forgiveness from God for letting my anger spill on her. "But I want a promise in return."

"Anything," she said, breathlessly. I knew she was starry-eyed at her own goodness.

"Promise me that you will pray every day for the Lord's swift return," I said, and hung up.

"That wasn't nice," Christ said. "She can't help it, and she had no idea what you meant."

"Well, *you* can help it," I cried. "Please come back *now* and save everyone from any more of this."

"Soon," he said, gently, as he has for two thousand years.

And then one day he said, "Come once more and see and experience holiness." He said it through the voice of my son-in-law, Andrew's father, who called to say that their second baby was on its way.

I went to the hospital and watched my daughter in labor. This is not easy, for a mother to see her daughter in pain. But we all did what we had been taught to do; and finally, they left the room with the doctor and the nurse who pushed the bed, Susan lying on her back, holding her husband's hand as he walked beside her.

I settled back in my chair, listening to my shoes shuffle on the beige tile, feeling the vinyl chair arms under my hands: I discovered that I was gripping tensely, and I let go and began to pray. Suddenly a nurse appeared, wearing her Martha scrub cap and gown.

"Your daughter would like for you to come too," she said. I followed, my heart dumb with gratitude, and I was gowned and masked and led to the darkened room where my son-in-law held up the back of Susan's bed and where everyone spoke in whispers.

"Now," said the doctor, aloud; and my daughter gave a small cry and was delivered of her second son.

He was laid on her stomach and massaged by both his parents.

"Adam," Susan whispered, seeing nobody but her husband and child.

"Adam Thomas?" asked my son-in-law, and they smiled, alone, exclusive, bound inexorably, wonderfully, in this process of making a new life.

"Here are your scissors, George," the doctor told my son-in-law. "You can cut the cord. Here."

I saw George's hand tremble. The baby's face was upturned, calm and splendid, his deep grey eyes fixed on heaven as his own father cut his umbilical cord.

Then they all looked at me as George laid his newest son in my arms.

"You can give him the warm bath," he said, still whispering; this was, of course, a Leboyer delivery. My own hands trembled as I slipped Adam Thomas into a pan full of warm saline water. The baby turned his head and let it rest on my bare wrist as I bathed him; and then he fell asleep.

"This is true holiness," said a voice, and I was confronted by Christ in my daughter's delivery room. I nodded, too full of what was happening this time to answer or argue.

Now, as I come to the end of this book, Adam Thomas is seven years old, and his big brother, Andrew, is nine. Adam knows how to take apart any mechanical object; he can start a car and program a computer; and Andrew can read everything: books, the newspapers, Bible stories, perhaps even Shakespeare, and he draws pictures of everything he sees. And they both call me on the telephone, crying, "Grandmother! Grandmother!" to say that their parents are serving liver again, or that they won a bicycle race, or telling long stories that only a grandmother will listen to, stories about fighting the good fight or catching the prize. I can still feel a warm, damp head against my wrist.

We are all now seven years older, Susan and George and my husband Ron, and I. Carol, clothed in shimmering creamy silk and wearing a circlet of fresh flowers in her hair, married Matthew; she walked down the aisle to "Sheep May Safely Graze," because she had come to love it as much as I. Frank and Kim, and their baby, Victor, live in an awesome atmosphere of art and music and love. They, all our children and grandchildren, and we, Ron and I, have had more love, more pain, and have become holier.

Visions assault my consciousness. I see the course of lives, mine and theirs and all people's: I see great trees of people, living and dying, crawling and walking, dancing and begging, making peace and causing wars. I see the history of human life, like a movie run too fast, backward and forward, and I cry out: O God! How can all of us, all of them, get to you? Are we holy enough by being born, with the breath of his life in us, or must we be made that way? Once saved always saved? Or saved repeatedly, continuously? Discipled, or converted? Deeds, or faith? Transcendence, or immanence? Black, or white?

"I see!" I cry, standing before my bedroom crucifix. The light dances on his silvery wounds. He looks at me with passionate interest.

"I see why you asked if there would be any faithful when you return," I said. "There are so many, all devising what they think are ways to love you or hate you."

He nods, still silent, listening for what it is I really want to say. Finally it comes out.

"I want everyone I love to go to heaven. I want Andrew and Adam and my children and my cleaning woman and my parents and everyone to go there. I want to write a book that tells everyone how to live forever with you," I say, by now letting my tears fall. "And I want to be with you. More than anything, that. I want to be with you."

The lips turn up into his irresistible smile. The paradoxes of my life, of all life, are under his Feet, below the cross. I watch to see if they will change into something less oppositional.

"Look up," he murmurs. "Look up at me."

I obey, my vision blurred with the tears of fear and of frustration and wondering and awe.

"It is not my will that any should perish," he says.

"But how do I really get to heaven?" I ask.

"You've written this whole book about it," he says.

"What?"

"Come on up on the cross with me," he says, and holds out his Hand.